Louis A. Banks

The People's Christ

A Volume of Sermons and Other Addresses and Papers

Louis A. Banks

The People's Christ
A Volume of Sermons and Other Addresses and Papers

ISBN/EAN: 9783337242527

Printed in Europe, USA, Canada, Australia, Japan

Cover: Foto ©Lupo / pixelio.de

More available books at **www.hansebooks.com**

TO

My Wife,

WHO HAS BEEN A SYMPATHETIC HELPMEET IN ALL
THE CARES OF MY MINISTRY,

This Volume

IS AFFECTIONATELY INSCRIBED.

CONTENTS.

	PAGE
INTRODUCTION. BY THE REV. CHARLES PARKHURST, D.D., EDITOR "ZION'S HERALD"	7

SERMONS.

I.	CHRIST'S WELCOME FOR THE CROWD	13
II.	CHRIST AND THE WORKING-MAN	31
III.	CHRIST AND THE WORKING-WOMAN	45
IV.	CHRIST AND THE SICK	61
V.	THE CHRISTIAN'S HORIZON	76
VI.	PETER AND HIS METHODS AT PENTECOST	87
VII.	OUR SISTER PHŒBE, THE DEACONESS	97
VIII.	SPIRITUAL NATURALIZATION	109
IX.	THE SOURCES OF AMERICAN NATIONAL LIFE,	119
X.	OUR BROTHER IN RED	134

SERMON FRAGMENTS.

I.	THE WRECKAGE AND SALVAGE OF MODERN CITIES	150
II.	CHRIST'S SYMPATHY FOR CITIES	155
III.	"IN DARKEST ENGLAND," WITH BOSTON APPLICATIONS	159
IV.	THE MISSION OF THE INKHORN	162

		PAGE
V.	THE VICTORY AND PROMISE OF AMERICAN PATRIOTISM	167
VI.	THE EXTRAVAGANCE AND BRUTALITY OF MODERN SPORTS	170
VII.	THE CAUSES OF SUICIDE	174
VIII.	THE AGE OF THE LIAR	177
IX.	THE STRUGGLE BETWEEN THE AMERICAN AND FOREIGN SABBATH	179
X.	NO MISSION TO GHOSTS	181

MISCELLANEOUS.

I.	HINDERANCES TO REVIVALS	184
	(An Address delivered at the Annual Meeting of the Evangelical Alliance of Boston, in Tremont Temple, January 14, 1889.)	
II.	NOWITKAN, THE HERMIT OF THE SKAGIT	193
III.	METHODISM AMONG THE NOOTSACKS	198
IV.	PERSONAL EXPERIENCES IN THE ANTI-CHINESE RIOTS	202
V.	THE LITTLE YELLOW MAN'S CLAIM ON THE AMERICAN CHRISTIAN	210
VI.	A SUNDAY WITH THE ANTI-CHINESE MOB IN SEATTLE	216

INTRODUCTION

TO be invited to a place beside the author of this volume, and to present him to the reading public, is a delightful privilege.

He is a notable co-worker with his ministerial brethren in the Christian Church. Therefore, to assist, in the slightest degree, in enlarging his sphere of usefulness, becomes a pleasurable duty. As he is a trusted and beloved friend, these lines are inspired by happy associations, and will be written with great frankness.

Rev. Louis Albert Banks, D.D., commands our approval as a minister of the gospel, because of certain strongly marked personal qualities.

His Serviceableness. — "The mind that was in Christ" is apprehended. The Master said, "I am among you as he that serveth;" and also, "Let him that is greatest among you be your servant." Dr. Banks has clearly caught this idea of service as the essence of the gospel of Christ. To serve the people, through his church as the channel of communication, is his absorbing purpose. To this end neither time, nor strength, nor any resources at his command, are spared. A single ambition possesses him, and that is to be a successful minister of Jesus Christ unto men. Combined with such devotion to his calling, there is utter indifference to the collateral honors and ecclesiastical preferments which are so highly esteemed and strongly coveted by many.

His Adaptability.—Rare are the men who so well understand the age and its needs, the people, and how to apply the gospel to them. He is a minister of the people, and presents the "People's Christ." The title of this volume is, therefore, fitly chosen. He ardently believes that the gospel is the power of God unto salvation, here and now.

The simplicity and strength of his faith are greatly to be envied. His glad confidence in the efficacy of this gospel for the reformation of the most debased, is never disturbed. Thoroughly has he diagnosed human life at the ordinary level, and he lives in closest sympathy with it. In his personal and church life he is ever bringing the power of the gospel in some new and impressive way to bear upon the people. He is made all things to all men, that he may by all means save some. In the glow of such consecration lies the secret, in no small degree, of the remarkable fertility of resources which he exhibits. Consecrated ingenuity is largely the result of concentration upon such a sublime purpose. He has a genius for the selection of topics for the pulpit. In studying the people and the newspapers, which are the best reflectors of current life and thought, with the Bible, so many subjects for pulpit treatment are suggested to him, that he is able to use but a small proportion of the whole number selected. How to reach the masses, is the question which most vexes the godly ministers of Christendom. Our friend has permanently solved the problem. The value of this volume to the Christian public will depend upon the degree to which Dr. Banks has made clear the way in which he presents Christ to the people, and his methods of work.

His Optimism. — We should most lamentably fail to portray our friend, if we did not mention the fact that he is one of the most hopeful and cheerful of men. In fraternal familiarity we have never had occasion to chide him except for incessant overwork. And yet he is always bubbling over with life and good cheer. He carries with him an inexhaustible supply of exuberance, which overflows to gladden every circle into which he enters. With his presence are associated the *bon mot*, the piquant repartee, and the heartiest good feeling. Gloom and melancholy must vanish when he appears. He makes no place for a religion of sighs and censure. His type of piety is healthy, vigorous, and always joyous. Not a little of the remarkable influence which he exerts upon the people is traceable to this attractive characteristic.

Is the interested reader of this volume anxious for a word even more personal concerning the preacher and his history?

At sixteen years of age he commenced to preach the gospel in Washington Territory, and many were converted. From seventeen to twenty-one, he taught school and studied law, being admitted to practise in the courts. He received his first regular appointment from Bishop Gilbert Haven, and was stationed at Portland, Oregon. Fearless as a reformer in his pulpit, he has been shot down by the infuriated saloonist, and mobbed by the anti-Chinese rioters. As the present pastor of St. John's Methodist Episcopal Church, South Boston, he has been favored with remarkable success. Thirty-five years of age, tall, of vigorous form, pleasant and intelligent face, never clerical but always frank, open-hearted, and manly, the reader would greatly enjoy a chat with him. Confident that such acquaintance with him, in his spirit, thought, and methods, as the perusal of this volume would impart, will be productive of good to the reader in making larger place for the Christ of the common people, we joyfully share in sending it forth to the general public.

CHARLES PARKHURST.

OFFICE OF ZION'S HERALD,
    Boston, Mass.

THE PEOPLE'S CHRIST

I

CHRIST'S WELCOME FOR THE CROWD

"And the apostles, when they returned, declared unto him what things they had done. And he took them, and withdrew apart to a city called Bethsaida. But the multitudes perceiving it followed him : *and he welcomed them*, and spake to them of the kingdom of God, and them that had need of healing he healed. And the day began to wear away; and the twelve came, and said unto him, Send the multitude away, that they may go into the villages and country round about, and lodge, and get victuals : for we are here in a desert place. But he said unto them, Give ye them to eat. And they said, We have no more than five loaves and two fishes; except we should go and buy food for all this people. For they were about five thousand men. And he said unto his disciples, Make them sit down in companies, about fifty each. And they did so, and made them all sit down. And he took the five loaves and the two fishes, and looking up to heaven, he blessed them, and brake; and gave to the disciples to set before the multitude. And they did eat, and were all filled: and there was taken up that which remained over to them of broken pieces, twelve baskets." — *Revised Version, Luke* ix. 10–17.

THIS picture brings out in strong coloring the attitude of Jesus toward the common people. He had gone aside into a quiet place for private conversation with his disciples. The multitude, perceiving this, were anxious and fearful lest he should escape them altogether.

There were among them many sick people, blind, and lame, and deaf, who had been attracted by the fame of the Saviour; and when they saw Jesus stealing away with his disciples, they doubtless felt as if their last hope was perishing. Life was a weary burden if healing and help were not found in Jesus. The Saviour's reception of them was characteristic. How easy it would have been to send back a committee of the disciples to inform the crowd that the Master was weary, needed rest, and desired to be alone with his intimate friends; and how natural from a human standpoint! But Jesus never saved himself at the expense of the poor and the suffering. He turns to them with words of welcome, talks with them of the kingdom of God, heals those who are sick, and when they are tired out and hungry turns the desert place into a picnic-ground for their comfort. May we not find a lesson in this picture for us to-day? The hope of the multitude now, as then, is in Jesus. Civilization and progress among the masses of the people must have motive-power from heaven. As ex-President Woolsey of Yale once said, "We might as well expect a locomotive to leave its place, and go safely across field and forest without steam or a road, as to hope for the upbuilding of society without the energizing power of Jesus Christ."

Our cities to-day are acknowledged by everybody to be centres of disorder and danger. Christianity must have some message of welcome and hope for the crowd. It is a very common thing, even among those who are accustomed to speak kindly of their individual acquaintances, to speak with contempt of humanity at large, as though it were a sort of common herd, unworthy of notice. Jesus had no petulance or contempt for the crowd. We have scarcely an instance recorded of his coming in contact with a large gathering of people, but what is added, "He had compassion on the multitude." The common people heard Jesus gladly. The poor found in him a brother. Then, as now, the great majority of men were poor. Until the coming of Jesus, to be poor and forced to toil with one's hands was to be a slave, not only in fact, but in the public mind. Christ made poverty no more a degradation. Mark Guy Pearse says, "Of all men who ever lived, Jesus Christ alone had any choice in the circumstances of his birth, and he chose the poorest lot and the hardest fare that ever befell any man. Henceforth poverty was no part of Divine disfavor. He who became poor was the wellbeloved Son, in whom the Father was well pleased. What wicked folly we utter when we talk as if the 'providential path' was always one where men made their fortunes, and as if we could measure God's goodness by the income. Jesus Christ took away the reproach of poverty. No more should any follower of Christ think poverty was dull, ignorant, unconscious, and incapable of any higher development, shut out from wisdom and grace and the sublimer aspect of things. But, alas! to-day the great example does not affect men's estimate of poverty. . . . Jesus Christ lowered the greatness of wealth by passing it by, and uplifted and hallowed the life of poverty by deliberately accepting it."

The entire life of Jesus tended to revolutionize the public estimate of the worth of humanity; that manhood, not titles, wealth, or power, were of supreme or even important worth.

If the Church of to-day is to be followed by the masses of men, it must have the same reverence for humanity, and the same brotherliness of spirit.

Well does Professor De Laveleye declare in the April *Forum:* "On the day that Christ said to the woman of Samaria, 'The hour cometh when ye shall neither in this mountain nor yet at Jerusalem worship the Father, but when true worshippers shall worship him in spirit and in truth,' was founded the true religion of humanity, the eternal and universal religion, irrespective of nationalities, doctrines, and dogmas.

The Sermon on the Mount can never be surpassed. In Christ's teachings worship and dogmas have very little place. The love of God as the type of all that is perfect, love for fellowmen, and charity to all, — this sums up the doctrine. 'Be ye therefore perfect, as my Father which is in heaven is perfect,' and 'Love thy neighbor as thyself;' on these commandments, are we not told, hang the law and the prophets? The poorer classes who have abandoned Christianity will return to it again when they have once been made to understand that it brings them equality and freedom; whereas atheism and materialism simply sanction their slavery, sacrificing them to certain pretended natural laws. The gospel of Christ, the 'good tidings' for the poor, would put an end to all our economic difficulties, if the spirit of brotherhood and charity therein taught were generally understood and practised."

I.

Jesus had a welcome for the heavily burdened and discouraged ones. So must we, his followers. The city and the whole land are full of burdened lives, — men and women who have fought in the battle of life and been worsted, who are disappointed and discouraged, who are out of employment and out of means, and know not where to turn to earn their bread. Some people imagine that every honest man or woman can readily find employment in this country. I once had a theory like that myself, — that it was only the lazy and the criminal that chose to be idle; but actual experience in the midst of the tide of the city has shattered my theory: it has gone down like a house built upon the sand.

Nothing has added to my heartache so much in the past few years as the efforts of honest men and women, who were true to God and their own consciences, spurning the bread that had the taint of the rum-traffic on it, yet unable for weeks at a time to find any employment.

A leading city journal vouches for this incident: —

"A respectable-appearing man was before the judge of the police court. 'Your honor,' said he, 'I am a fair mechanic, and have been in this city several weeks unable to find work. My money is gone, and I can find nothing to do. I have been willing to work, but no one whom I found would give me any. I cannot beg, and [here the tears came to his eyes], Judge, I won't steal. For God's sake send me somewhere, anywhere, where I will be out of the cold. I can't sleep at the stations, and I don't want to.'

"'Well, my good man,' said the justice, 'I

can only send you to the jail, and in order to do so you must be charged with disorderly conduct.'

"'I suppose, your honor, it is disorderly conduct to be as poor as I am.'

"'That is not what I mean,' said the justice; 'I only want to be fair and just with you.'

"'Just and fair; that's it, your honor. This world is given to justice and fairness. When I ask for work, they tell me that they have none. If I ask for bread, I am called a tramp. I am glad there is some one here who wants to be fair and just.'

"'Well,' said the justice, ' I will place a fine of thirty dollars against you, which will give you two months in the house of correction, where at least you will be warm and have enough to eat.'

"'God bless you, Judge!' was the prisoner's response; and he was taken back down-stairs."

What a commentary is an incident like that on our present social system!

Well does the editor of the *Christian Union* say: "The time will come when it will be thought amazing that a Christian State should ever have existed that provided self-supporting labor for a thief, and refused to provide it for an honest man. Poverty is not a crime. Inability to earn a living is not a crime. No wonder that under a system which treats them as crimes, crime increases."

The most recent statistics show that we have nearly, or quite, 500,000 criminals in the United States; of this 500,000, more than one-third, or 167,000, are under twenty years of age; that more than 250,000 are under twenty-one years of age; and that more than 333,000 are under twenty-two years of age.

The Christian Church must do something more than stand back aghast at these figures. It must have some message of hope and welcome toward a better life for these young men and women who are being overthrown and destroyed by the fiercest temptations known to humanity.

There is a conviction on the part of a vast majority of laboring, burdened men and women, that the churches are selfish, caring only for their own interests. However unfounded this conviction may be in many instances, the fact remains. The burden lies upon the church to overcome this conviction and remove it by the warmth of its sympathy and welcome.

An English clergyman writing in the *Nineteenth Century* gives this reason why the poorer working people do not go to church: "They see the churches well built and nearly always shut up; they see the public houses, towering above their own small houses, blazing at every turn, and always open; they see their own small rooms, often badly built, always too small for even their little furniture and often large families."

Now, is not that a good picture of what exists in Boston? Here are a few scores of churches nearly always shut up. From two to three days in the week would be a high average for the time they are open.

On the other hand, there are hundreds of saloons open all the time.

There is a need of a revolution in our use of our church buildings. No business firm could exist and waste its resources as do most of our churches. I hope to live to see the day when this church, and every other church like it in our towns and cities, shall stand open day and night, lighted and warmed, full of welcome and hope, a veritable beacon-light to every poor and oppressed man or woman on our streets.

A brother clergyman gives this suggestive incident in the *Methodist Times* of London: —

"Some time ago I was going down a main thoroughfare of the city in which I then resided, when I saw some twenty or thirty men who were at work in some way about the road, laying drains, or something of that sort. It was the dinner-hour, and there in the pelting rain they sat eating their provision, — about as dreary and cheerless a set as one could see. In that road within a mile there were no less than five places of worship; but the very nearest was that of which I was then the minister. I at once got the schoolroom opened, and bade the men welcome, promised it should be at their service so long as they were anywhere near, and had a fire at which they could warm their coffee and themselves. I told them that they were at perfect liberty to smoke after dinner; but the whole time not a man lit his pipe within the walls: it was the instinct of a true gentleman awakened by a little act of kindness. When their work lay further down the road, another place was similarly opened to receive them. Now comes the interesting part of the story. On the Sunday some of these men walked a long way and endured the infliction of a sermon from me, because, as one explained, 'You see, one good turn deserves another.' I certainly much appreciated the kindness of that good turn. Of this be sure, though it was so little a matter, — a cost of half a crown for extra cleaning covering the whole outlay, — those men will henceforth carry a more kindly feeling towards the religion of Jesus Christ."

Only by a like appeal to the common brotherhood of the masses of men and women can we hope to win them to the Church, and through the Church to our Saviour and King.

II.

Jesus had a welcome for sinners. I do not mean respectable, titled, high-toned, wealthy, powerful sinners, whom most people flatter and fawn upon, but disgraced, unknown, friendless sinners.

For illustration, remember the poor sinful woman who was about to be stoned to death by the mob, and Jesus mildly said, " Let him that is without sin cast the first stone." They all slunk away, like the cowards they were. Jesus turned to the woman with a hopeful word, " Go, and sin no more."

Or, that other case when Jesus had been invited to dinner at the house of the rich Pharisee, and a wicked woman of the town, but penitent for her sin, came into his presence, and washed his feet with her tears, and wiped them with the hairs of her head. I want to say a word of justice for those Pharisees; for, do you know, I think they showed more patience and forbearance than the average dinner-party in Boston would show if the same scene were to be reproduced in our time. True, they were shocked and astonished, and questioned the propriety of it; but we do not read that one of them left the room.

Does anybody believe that from a company of our modern society people, even in religious circles, there would not have been a more emphatic protest against such a "vulgar" proceeding?

Nothing is in stronger contrast between the spirit of Jesus and much of our modern Christianity, than our indifference to the salvation of this class of sinful but immortal souls. Society is cruelly unjust. It stretches out its hand to the sinning man who has led his sister woman down to ruin, but almost boastfully speaks of shutting the "iron door" against his victim. But there was no iron door between Jesus and these poor, sinful souls. I do press it upon the hearts of Christian women, that it is your imperative duty to hold out a Christ-like hand of welcome and of hope to every penitent fallen woman.

Multitudes in our churches are always expressing a desire to do something for Jesus, yet refusing every practical opportunity. Margaret Preston paints a sad but suggestive poetic picture, that is very true to life: —

"If I had dwelt," — so mused a tender woman,
   All fine emotions stirred
Through pondering o'er that Life, divine yet human,
   Told in the Sacred Word, —

CHRIST'S WELCOME FOR THE CROWD

"If I had dwelt of old, a Jewish maiden,
    In some Judæan street
Where Jesus walked, and heard His word so laden
    With comfort strangely sweet, —

"And seen the face where utmost pity blended
    With each rebuke of wrong,
I would have left my lattice, and descended
    And followed with the throng.

"If I had been the daughter, jewel-girdled,
    Of some rich rabbi there;
Seeing the sick, blind, halt, my blood had curdled
    At sight of such despair;

"And I had wrenched the sapphires from my fillet,
    Nor let one spark remain;
Snatched up my gold, amid the crowd to spill it,
    For pity of their pain;

"I would have let the palsied fingers hold me;
    I would have walked between
The Marys and Salome, while they told me
    About the Magdalene.

"'Foxes have holes,' — I think my heart had broken
    To hear the words so said;
While Christ had not — were sadder ever spoken?—
    'A place to lay His head!'

"I would have flung abroad my doors before Him,
    And in my joy have been
First on the threshold, eager to adore Him,
    And crave His entrance in!"

Ah, would you so? Without a recognition,
    You passed Him yesterday;
Jostled aside, unhelped, His mute petition,
    And calmly went your way.

With warmth and comfort garmented and girdled,
    Before your window-sill
Sweep heart-sick crowds — and if your blood is curdled,
    You wear your jewels still.

You catch aside your robes, lest want should clutch them
    In its implorings wild;
Or lest some woeful penitent might touch them,
    And you be thus defiled.

O dreamers, dreaming that your faith is keeping
    All service free from blot!
Christ daily walks your streets, sick, suffering, weeping,
    And ye perceive Him not!

"He that hath ears to hear, let him hear."

The great demand of the hour is for the Church to get and keep the heart of the common people. The future of this and every age is in the hands of the toiling multitudes, and not the privileged few.

Jesus proved to John his divinity by "preaching the gospel to the poor." Let us follow in the footsteps of our Master.

I love the Methodist Church. I am thankful to God for her history and her victories; she has no more loyal son in all her borders. And my highest ambition for Methodism is that she shall keep true to her Master, and keep close to the throbbing hearts of the people.

Nearly all our converts, in the early years of Methodism, were from the poorest class of daily toilers; and throughout our whole history we have had greatest success when we have been true to our mission and kept close to the heart of the common people.

At a great Wesleyan missionary meeting in London, the Rev. Thomas Champness related a suggestive incident. A number of years ago there was a family of farmers in the north of England; they were not prosperous, and were so poor that the sons emigrated. The only daughter went out to seek a situation. She became, not a governess, not a companion, but a straightforward, honest servant girl. This girl felt it a nobler thing to go and work in a big town and earn wages as a servant girl than to idle at home; and one day, when she was cleaning the steps, a bricklayer fellow came up. He saw this nice girl cleaning the steps, and he said, "I must see her again." So he managed to find out what place of worship she went to, and it turned out to be the Methodist chapel, and so he said, "I'll go there." When he went there for something he liked, he got something he did not like; he found out he was a sinner needing a Saviour. He also found out that this girl did not much care to talk to him so long as his heart was not right with God. He gave himself to Jesus Christ, and then asked her if he might come and see her a bit, and so " they made it up." I suppose there is a more euphonious way of expressing it, but you understand what I mean. They got married, and he worked at his trade for some time. He kept on saving money, till by and by he said, "I shall build a house for myself." His ambition was to have a house fit to receive the Methodist preachers. He built this house, and when it was finished he took his wife and children in a sort of beautiful procession to enter it *via* the front door, and when he got there he said to his wife, "Do you see those steps?" And she said, "I do." "Those were the steps thee wert cleaning when I first saw thee. The master's house was pulled down, and I went to the auction and bought the steps. I said, 'When thee hast a house of thine own, these steps shall be in the front;'" and up those steps have walked Dr. Newton, Dr. Bunting, and the great and mighty men of the Methodist past — those steps that that woman cleaned. It is too long a story to tell, but her son went into business with his father — a smart Methodist lad and local preacher — and he said one day to his father, "We mustn't always be working like this; we must make some more money. Why shouldn't we buy a clay-field and make our own bricks?" The father said, "Very well," and they bought a field of clay which turned out to be a very mine of gold. Some of the best bricks in England were made there; it made their fortune. And the son of the woman who cleaned the steps became one of the greatest financial bulwarks of the English Methodism of his day.

God will take care of the Church which cares for the girl that cleans the steps.

A few years ago our Methodist papers were ringing with deserved tributes to David Preston, the Methodist banker and philanthropist, of Detroit. Ministers from half a dozen States attended his funeral, and he was carried to his grave like the prince he was. Thirty-eight years before, David Preston entered Detroit on foot, a homeless lad, twelve dollars in debt, and went to work at twelve dollars a month. Some Methodist preacher looked after the poor boy, and made him welcome to his humble place of worship. Little did that preacher dream that he was giving welcome to a coming man, who should, out of his liberality, give to Methodism one of its greatest churches in the nation, and whose shoulder should be under every great burden the denomination was to lift for a quarter of a century.

The hope of Methodism for the future is in the railroad shops, the iron foundries, the factories, the stores, the places of toil where laboring boys and girls are earning their bread.

May God fill our own hearts with a spirit of

welcome, until it shall be impossible for anybody to live on this South Boston peninsula without knowing that every toiling man, woman, and child is not only welcome to the best we have, but is earnestly sought after and desired.

The Church is not to be a fortress manned by a self-indulgent band, seeking only refuge and ease and salvation for themselves, but rather a marching army, keeping step to the bugle-notes of Jesus. "Go out quickly into the streets and lanes of the city, and bring in hither the poor, and maimed, and blind, and lame." And yet again: "Go out into the highways and hedges, and constrain them to come in, that my house may be filled."

II.

CHRIST AND THE WORKING-MAN [1]

"Come unto me, all ye that labor and are heavy laden, and I will give you rest. Take my yoke upon you, and learn of me, for I am meek and lowly of heart, and ye shall find rest unto your souls. For my yoke is easy, and my burden is light." — *Matt.* ii. 28-30.

WHAT is Christianity worth to Boston? That is the question we are to ask and ponder in this series of discourses. What is Christianity doing to make the lives of men and women and children happier and nobler than they would be without it? The question is not, what has Christianity done for the race at large, not what impulse has it given to civilization in general, but rather, what is it doing to help the phases of human need that present themselves to the people of Boston, in the year of our Lord 1890? The appeal must be to the facts. When the disciples of John came to Jesus, desiring to know if he was the Messiah, he threw them back upon the facts which appealed to their own eyes and ears: "Go show John the things ye do see

---

[1] The three following discourses were delivered in a series of sermons on "Christianity in Boston."

and hear; the blind receive their sight, the lame walk, the lepers are cleansed, the deaf hear, the dead are raised up, and the poor have the gospel preached unto them." The appeal must be the same to-day. We must search the living facts, and not past traditions, for the answer. Every age must produce its own evidences of Christianity.

I invite you, for a few Sunday evenings, to pursue with me a frank and earnest investigation of the evidences of Christianity; not as they appear in the learned tomes of the scholar's library, but as they appear in the churches, homes, schools, workshops, hospitals, and complicated network of the daily life of the people that make up this bustling human hive which we call Boston.

Coming then to our first theme, "Christ and the Working-man," I invite you to notice the daring invitation of Jesus to the toilers of earth: "Come unto me, all ye that labor and are heavy laden, and I will give you rest. Take my yoke upon you, and learn of me, for I am meek and lowly of heart, and ye shall find rest unto your souls. For my yoke is easy, and my burden is light."

That was a brave challenge. Jesus stood in the midst of the burden-bearers of Palestine. The majority, there as everywhere, were poor working people. Jesus looked over this crowd of burden-bearers — women with heavy water-pots on shoulder or head, men bending under loads of fuel or fish or merchandise, people who knew what burdens meant, and what it was to be tired from overloading — and he uttered this bold challenge. They were words of real prophecy, if you take them in the most earthly and literal sense only. Think of it as you go out into the street to-night, as you look up through the clear white electric light, and consider how much better it is for the laboring men of Boston to have the benefit of that splendid illumination, rather than to be compelled to carry each man his own torch, or his little lamp fastened around his ankle, that he may find his path through the darkness. Think of it when you enter your home, and open the faucet, and the pure water bursts out of the wall at your touch, as it burst from the desert rock of old, under the rod of Moses. Think of it, and thank God for the challenge of Jesus!

The miracles of Judæa are the every-day experience of Christian Boston. But remember, it is only the cities which have come under the touch of Christianity, that have made these giant strides in the arts of life. Let us look around us, and see in what other way Christ is manifesting his sympathy with the working-men of Boston.

Here, for example, is a young man who came down last week from the old farm in Vermont, or from the carpenter shop in St. John, N. B., and it may be, for the sake of the dear name of your old town, that you are half homesick for, you have come in here to St. John's Church to-night. You are to be a working-man in Boston. You have your two hands, your honest purpose, and your clean blood, inherited from good, honest, hard-working parents, for capital.

Don't undervalue that capital. Franklin, Lincoln, Garfield, Grant, and a host of others, have stored up an inexhaustible bank account with the American people, with no other capital to begin with than that. You are here to face the new world of the city, to earn your bread, to win a home, to live your life, to do the best for yourself, to fill your place in your age. Now what does Christianity do to meet you as a young working-man, that ought to attract your attention, awaken your interest, and arouse your gratitude? Well, in the first place, my brother, Christianity has built this church, lighted it with welcome, and hung its cards of invitation on the streets, that you might see them and come in. It stationed me in the corridor, that, at the very threshold, you might have a hand-shake of brotherhood and a word of cheer. It stations me in this pulpit, and the choir in yonder gallery, that you, taking up these new burdens on your untried shoulders, might be soothed in spirit, inspired with hope, and comforted with the knowledge of God's sympathy and presence.

If you had been in Rome, or Athens, or Jerusalem, before the days of Jesus, a strange carpenter, or blacksmith, or teamster, such a welcome as this would have been impossible; as indeed it would be impossible to-day, in any city on earth, that has not come largely under the sway of the Man of Galilee. And yet this is only one of the two hundred and fifty Protestant churches, alone, that stand like beacon lights along the coast of the city's life. In addition to these, there are thirty-four Catholic churches, which set a good example for us Protestants in one thing at least, that they are open every day in the week.

But what else has Christianity to say to the young man that has just come to Boston? On the corner of Boylston and Berkeley Streets stands the hall of the Young Men's Christian Association. A mansion it is, standing among the princely mansions of the Back Bay, but differing from them in this, that the humblest young man who breaks rock on the Boston streets for his daily bread, is made as welcome to the fellowship of that beautiful young men's home, as the son of wealth and luxury. Here are books and papers. Here are innocent games under healthful surroundings. Here is a splendid gymnasium for physical exercise under skilled teachers. Above all, here are cleanly yet genial associations. You are lonesome, you are heart-hungry for friendship. The worst sickness in the world is homesickness, and the loneliest spot on earth is a city crowded full of people none of whom take the slightest interest in you. But here, in this Young Men's Christian Association, you may meet young men of your own age, of your own trade, under the most pleasant conditions, and yet without temptation to evil. Here, too, are schools for instruction. You had to leave school, it may be, before the education you had marked out for yourself was complete, in order to relieve the pressure on the dear shoulders of an overworked father or mother. Here in the evening, after a day's work is over, you may carry on a course of intellectual development that will go far to make up to you the loss of the college course that once filled your boyhood's dreams. Here you may hear instructive lectures and soul-inspiring concerts.

Up on Boylston Street stands the Young Men's Christian Union building, another magnificent palace with luxurious appointments that no palace on earth possessed before Jesus began to lift men's burdens, and broaden the horizon of their thinking. All that I have said of the first of these splendid Christian homes for young men, is true of the second. Something of the magnitude of this work for young men accomplished by these central homes may be gathered from the fact that, from October to March of last year, over seven hundred young men visited Association Hall every day. One thousand young men were members of the gymnasium, and over nine hundred registered for the evening classes.

Both of these young men's homes have employment bureaus connected with them in order to increase the opportunity of helping that most lonesome of all young men — the one who is out of work in a strange city. Nearly nine hundred were thus helped to positions last year. In the lecture courses, such men as Phillips Brooks, Edward Everett Hale, Robert Collyer, William Lloyd Garrison, Reuen Thomas, Professor Atkinson, Joseph Cook, and others scarcely less famous, have appeared, while the best singers and concert companies of the land have furnished entertainment. In fact, Christianity, by the founding and support of these centres for the young men of Boston, — forums for the development of physical, social, intellectual, and moral manhood, and the branches of these institutions in various parts of the city, — makes it easier and cheaper in dollars and cents, and in outlay of energy, for a young working-man of Boston to become a cultivated, intelligent Christian gentleman, than it is to haunt the dime museums, or play pool and be a fool. And this is not all.

Perhaps the exigencies of life in youth have been such that you have not been able to acquire any accurate knowledge of the trade you desire to follow. Christian thoughtfulness does not fail you here. On Washington Street, in the heart of the city, stands the Wells Memorial Institute for working-men, born of intelligent Christian philanthropy. Here you may attend free lectures on carpentry, lectures for practical electricians; and, if you will permit me to make a suggestion, I will say that the most promising field for successful adventure which lies before the brainy young working-man to-day, is the domain of electricity. In this working-men's institute you may find free instruction on steam and engineering. Here, again, as in the Young Men's Association, you will find concerts and lectures for general instruction and education. A working-men's club, a working-men's bank, and a system to secure co-operative discount in purchase of fuel and flour, are further characteristics of the Wells Memorial Institute. The institution recently devised by Mr. Paine, in Roxbury, promises to pursue these general lines into still wider fields.

But the time goes on. I turn now to a man who came here to work fifteen years ago. You have fought your way as best you could. You have joined hands with some honest workingwoman, and established yourself, if not in a house of your own, at least in your own hired house. Little children are growing up around you; they need instruction. You are busy all day long, and the wife's hands are full to overflowing with household cares. Who shall teach them to read and write? Who shall open to them the great stores of human knowledge, and make all the streams of human wisdom tributary to their successful voyage? What has Boston's Christian civilization to say to you now? Right royally does our fair city stand this test. Palatial school buildings are waiting in answer, — school buildings such as children never saw before in the history of the race. These magnificent educational temples stand with wide-open doors, welcoming the workingmen's boys and girls. Not only so, but, miracle of thoughtfulness! an array of skilled teachers stand with free text-books in their hands, ready not only to welcome your children at the threshold of knowledge, but to put, as it were, a premium on its pursuit.

As they grow older, and new books of reference are needed, or in the long winter evenings you desire to forget your toil and keep your mind fresh and strong, in touch with the affairs of the ever-new world, behold, the great Public Library, with its branches stretching out on every hand, is offering the use of its wealth of priceless books, without money and without price.

Have you lost your situation, and seek employment? The Appleton Industrial Home, with great-hearted Dr. A. J. Gordon at its head, helped more than twelve thousand working people last year to employment, while nearly every church is to some extent an employment bureau, and nearly every Christian pastor is many times a year glad to serve as an employment agent.

But perhaps misfortune comes, the family are sick for weary weeks, possibly for months; it is impossible to make the ends meet in the daily rounds of household economy. What does Christian Boston do to meet this emergency? The churches lead first with a larger or smaller fund, from every one of their two hundred and eighty-four centres in the city. Lodges and mutual benefit associations, — all of which owe the germ of whatever usefulness they have developed to the spirit of Christianity which commands that every man look not on his own things alone, but also on the things of others, — follow their example. To give comfort and sympathy, as well as assistance, in this hour of misfortune, the Associated Charities, with its centre in Chardon Street, and its branch conference in every section of the city, finds its mission. The Associated Charities undertakes to break the isolation and loneliness of these days of hardship by the personal visitation of men and women of kindly heart (for no others will forsake their selfish ways to take up this work of Christly self-denial), who seek by counsel and encouragement, and by securing temporary relief when it is needed, to save the overworked and disappointed toiler from despair, and brace up the courage for a new struggle against life's difficulties. Working in connection with the Associated Charities, and granting such relief as it finds to be necessary, is the Provident Association, which last year gave temporary relief, after personal visitation, to over two thousand working-men's families, comprising nearly eight thousand individuals. In addition to this, good men and women for more than a hundred years, moved upon by the spirit of Christian kindness, have been setting apart for the relief of the poor and unfortunate, certain funds which are held in trust by the overseers of the poor. These funds amount to-day to over six hundred and seventy-five thousand dollars in the general fund, besides which there is the Firemen's Relief Fund of one hundred and eight thousand dollars, and the Police Charitable Fund of two hundred thousand dollars more.

Indeed, there stands to-day invested, for the benefit of the working people of Boston, in these public funds alone, a grand total, — one million, seven hundred and sixty-six thousand, four hundred and seventy dollars, and ninety-nine cents. Time would fail me to tell of the Howard Benevolent Society, which in its generous history has distributed over three hundred thousand dollars; of the Roxbury Charitable Society; of the Relief Corps work of the Grand Army of the Republic, and many other less noted, but in the sight of Jesus none the less worthy efforts to relieve the working-man in the hour of misfortune and trouble. Even in a childless old age he may find a safe haven in the Old Couples' Home at Egleston Square, or the Home for Aged Men on Springfield Street.

I am deeply conscious that the Christian people of Boston are doing by no means all that they might or ought to do, to show their sympathetic feeling for working-men, but let us thank God that so much is being done, and take courage for the future.

But in all that I have said, I have not mentioned Christ's greatest benediction on the working-man. When Jesus walked among men, to heal the sick, to open the eyes of the blind, and give health to the leper, was not his great mission. These were only incidental to his chief mission, which was to open the eye of the soul, to cleanse the evil heart, and to comfort and give peace to the wounded, broken spirit. I have no figures to show, and no figures can show, what Christ is doing to-day, in Boston, for the working-man who yields to him his whole heart and love. To such a man Jesus is more than all else. He is his daily companion. The shop becomes glorified because Christ is there. The home becomes sacred as a training-school for heaven, because Jesus dwells there a beloved Guest. And in dark hours, when sickness creeps upon the household, and the shadow of death falls on the little lambs of the home flock, Jesus stands by the working-man's side, and lays the strong, kindly hand of the brotherly carpenter on his shoulder, and says, "Suffer little children to come unto me, . . . for of such is the kingdom of heaven." And when his own arm trembles, and his eye grows dim, and the loneliness of his coming departure steals over him, the same sweet voice that has cheered him in the shop, and soothed him in the home, whispers again, "In my Father's house are many mansions; I go to prepare a place for you; I will come again, and receive you unto myself, that where I am, there ye may be also."

III

CHRIST AND THE WORKING-WOMAN

"Jesus, therefore, being wearied with his journey, sat thus by the well. It was about the sixth hour. There cometh a woman of Samaria to draw water." — *John* iv. 6, 7.
"And upon this came his disciples, and they marvelled that he was speaking with a woman." — *John* iv. 27.

THIS is the way cities were watered in those days. The cities and towns were built on the hilltops, for the purposes of defence; and up these rocky hillsides all the water was carried by women, in water-skins or stone jars. It is a far cry from the well of Sychar, and its daily train of women laden with water-skins, to the Chestnut Hill reservoir, and the faucet in every attic, but no farther than the uplift Christ has given to womanhood.

There is nothing more striking in the contrasts of civilization than the superiority of the position of woman under the reign of Christianity, compared with any other system the world has ever known. The recognition of woman's equality in the struggle of life, however, seems to be a flower which demands a high state of cultivation in the intellectual and moral soil of humanity.

Down in the south-western territories there is a huge species of century-plant called the Maguey. It is covered with great thick leaves, a foot wide, two inches thick, and sometimes ten feet in length. This plant, which in large sections of the country is almost the sole native agricultural product, is long-lived and ugly, and armed with the sharpest thorns. Out of its juice the Mexicans make a most stupefying liquor, called "pulque." Revolting enough seems this great forest of ill-starred plants, until suddenly, within a few weeks, from the midst of these homely leaves, there will shoot up a shaft twenty feet in height, which will crown itself with a wreath of beautiful flowers. This possibility of beauty was in the plant through all the years of its ugliness. It only waited the proper conditions to bring it forth. So there has been in Christianity, from the beginning, this pledge of woman's right to an equal place with man in the world's workshop. Through all the dreary bondage of the dark ages, unsuspected for the most part, it was lying there in the words of Jesus as well as in the whole spirit and philosophy of the New Testament.

It is only in the present century, however, that Christ's recognition of womanhood has come to have general influence and power, even in nominally Christian lands. There are people now living who can remember when in Boston there were less than a score of branches of occupation open to women, and when there was not a college in America, or in the world, which gave women an equal chance for education with men. This advance has been largely hastened by the self-sacrificing devotion of a few earnest souls who refused to read into the Bible the sex aristocracy which the selfishness and prejudices of mankind had imputed to it. Notable among these is Lucy Stone, of the *Woman's Journal.* I always thank God, in remembrance of her, in recognition of the wider sphere which she has largely helped to open to my own sisters, and to the whole army of working-women throughout the land. Some day, when her work is done, the women of America will build her a monument on Boston Common; but her noblest monument will be the wider opportunity for usefulness given to hundreds of thousands of hopeful young lives.

So marvellous has been the advance of the recognition of woman's right to do whatever she can do well, that in 1885 there were in Massachusetts 4,467 branches of occupation in which women were engaged or employed. There is, however, one point of gross injustice to which women are subjected, to which repeated attention must be called, until justice is done. It is still largely true that women are paid, not according to their work, but according to their sex. In Boston, the school committee set the example in the treatment of teachers, and the large dry-goods houses follow in their wake. There is, and can be, no valid excuse for this. And every good man and woman ought to utter their protest against this vestige of unreasoning prejudice.

Now, turning from the general treatment of the subject, let us see in what way Christianity is practically making it easier for working-women to be true, and noble, and happy.

First, on Berkeley and Appleton Streets, there is the Young Women's Christian Association, the first mission of which is to supply the lack of a home, and to give pure and congenial associations to working-women, especially among the younger class, who find themselves alone or strangers in the city. This society employs a missionary, who frequently meets young girls at the railroad stations and steamboat landings, and gives them the directions which young women often find very helpful on arrival in a strange city. This travellers' aid matron says, "I am often fully repaid for any effort when a young woman says, 'I don't know what I should have done without you.'"

During the past year, 1,224 girls, in this hour of loneliness and confusion, have had their hearts gladdened by the presence of a Christian woman, wearing the badge of the Young Women's Christian Association, who, in the name of Jesus, was seeking for them, and glad to render them the very help they needed. In the 1,224 thus assisted, many being without friends were brought to the Association, and work found for them. Many others were accompanied to their friends in distant parts of the city, or suburban towns; others were taken to railroad stations and put on their respective trains, the precaution being often taken of speaking to the conductor in their behalf, or telegraphing to their friends. It would seem strange that any young woman, thus helped, could ever again hear the name of Christ without a quicker heart-beat of gratitude. More than three hundred young women are in the boarding homes of the society; five hundred more find innocent and healthful recreation in a gymnasium prepared for their use. The Association has established schools for the purpose of preparing young women for wider spheres of usefulness in home and business circles, training them to become skilled workers in whatever direction they may be inclined. There is a school of cookery, a training school for servants, a school for stenography and typewriting, together with additional classes for commercial and industrial and domestic education, such as dressmaking, etc.

For women who are out of employment, the kindly hand of this Young Women's Christian Association has been a great boon. That you may know something of the magnitude of the help thus rendered, let me give you the number and classes of working-women who were assisted to employment last year: 191 nurses, 143 attendants, 53 companions to invalids, 15 superintending housekeepers, 114 working housekeepers, 306 seamstresses, 17 matrons, 17 infant nurses, 37 nursery seamstresses, 26 bookkeepers, 40 governesses, 2,099 domestics, 103 miscellaneous, — making a total of 3,161 working-women who thus found a friend in need.

Again, on Boylston Street, facing the Public Garden, stands the Woman's Educational and Industrial Union. Here any working-woman, day or evening, may be sure of finding sympathy and friendship and protection against injustice. In addition to giving women a chance to sell the products of their labor, there is one feature of the work of this Union which is especially unique and praiseworthy. This is its protective department, the object of which is to obtain for working-women wages which have been wrongfully withheld. A number of leading lawyers nobly give their services free of charge to this department, and thus make it possible for the complaints of working-women who are too poor to employ legal services, to be thoroughly investigated, and if worthy to be prosecuted to a just issue. The very existence of this society acts as a pressure upon mean employers, and is a wall of defence to the poor working-woman. The Woman's Educational and Industrial Union also provides lectures, classes, and entertainments.

It has "Mothers' Meetings," and "Talks with Young Girls" from women of broad experience and high reputation. Its endeavor is to make the Union a centre of local information, and to afford opportunities for interchange of thought on questions of vital importance to women. It investigates fraudulent advertisements, and publicly warns women against them. It also procures situations for the unemployed, whenever possible. Many hundreds of working-women, unable, because of household cares, to work outside of their own homes, find sale for home-cooked food, and useful and fancy articles, in the Union's salesrooms. At the lunch-room, soups, tea, coffee, and chocolate are offered at moderate prices. Working-women carrying their own lunches are always welcome. The president says, "The Union stands on broad principles. It is wholly unsectarian. It believes in the religion of human kinship, mutual helpfulness, and of obligation to live for the truth, with love toward all. Any thought which will aid in such living is welcomed, from whatever source. Another of our principles is that we meet on a basis no narrower than humanity. Not that all are equals; there is no such thing as general equality; but in every human being there is something akin to something in every other one. The deep things of the heart, the realities of existence, are common to all. The Union invites all, that each may receive help according to her needs."

Another outgrowth of Christian sentiment and sympathy is the Boston Association of Working-Girls' Clubs. There are now twelve of these clubs in the different parts of the city and immediate vicinity. Perhaps this little picture, from the Amaranth Club of Roxbury, may give you some idea of what they are like. This club-room is in the immediate vicinity of Prang's, Fiedler's, and other factories in Roxbury, so that the membership is largely made up from working-girls from these factories. In May last, the club had a membership of eighty. The rooms are open every evening except Sunday. Classes were formed in cooking, dressmaking, millinery, embroidery, and singing.

An enthusiastic committee of Roxbury ladies furnished the rooms, and arranged the multifarious details of these many branches of instruction, while younger ladies helped the social element, wiping out by their own graciousness and cordiality any class distinctions among the members of the club. They form with the girls a hospitality committee, who take turns in introducing new-comers, and in furthering social pleasures.

One evening in the week is given to music, games, and conversation. They plan together for little receptions and re-unions and mothers' teas and the like. The parlor is made as attractive as possible, with piano, bright lights, pictures, curtains, bookcase, settees, chairs, and all necessary appliances. The girls find this a pleasant refuge after the long day's din at the factory. Entering pale and tired, they go home with a happy "Good-night, all," or "I have had a splendid time." Large-hearted Christian women, who have means to spare, ought to see to it that this happy thought bears abundant fruit in the multiplication of these working-girls' clubs in every section of the city.

For the past thirteen years there has existed in Boston the Massachusetts Society for the University Education of Women, which, it seems to me, is peculiarly suggestive of the advancing

Christian spirit of our time. Let me give you a single example of this society's work. A young woman attending the Boston University was brought to the attention of the committee of this society. An investigation showed that she was clearly overworked and underfed. The secretary says of her: "One might as well have objected to the dome remaining on the State House, as to that girl remaining in college. There she was. Cold and hunger and hard work made no difference — there she intended to stay. She was given financial help, sufficient to free her from the necessity of earning money during term time, and the committee tried to relieve her from as much outside work as possible. In spite of care, however, her health began to weaken, and it seemed unwise for her to continue her college course. The faculty and the committee argued and debated the question; they urged and exhorted the girl. To all their efforts she opposed the most adamantine determination. 'What if I am sick?' she calmly queried. 'Wouldn't it be better to die trying to do something, than to live after proving myself incapable of good work?' A girl's morbid fancy, if you please to call it so, but what can be done about it? It is one of those cases in which it is useless to deprecate the ambition and the determination. There they are: all that can be done is to recognize them.

"Back to college came this determined young woman, with her courage as undaunted and her purse as thin as ever, but, we are glad to add, with her health much improved by the long vacation. Yet hardly can we call those weeks a vacation, during which she studied enough to make up her deficient examinations, and earned money for her winter clothing. She lives in a cheap room in the suburbs; by some light labor she earns her board and a little spending money; the University provides her tuition, and the loan library of this society furnishes her books. The girl is now well and happy, proud of her successes, cheerily independent, and more determined than ever to have a college education."

One young woman who was aided by the society is now helping to lift up her degraded sisters in India; another is helping to bring a better civilization to the little olive-colored women of China; one is making excellent progress in a medical school; one occupies a professor's chair in a college; many are teaching in prominent schools and academies; while a large number are extending their influence through the channels of home, and are giving to their little children the results of the cultured womanhood they acquired by aid of this Christian thoughtfulness.

For women in poverty and misfortune, the Associated Charities, the Provident Association, the Howard Benevolent Society, and the funds under the care of the overseers of the poor, to which special reference was made in the first discourse of this series, have the same kindly relation to working-women. Besides these, there is the Home for Aged Women at 108 Revere Street, the Roxbury Home for Children and Aged Women on Burton Avenue, the Winchester Home Corporation at No. 10 Eden Street, and the Home for Aged Colored Women at No. 27 Myrtle Street. Each of these homes ministers most gently to aged working-women, who in their old age, when no longer able to work, find themselves without the friendly aid of children or other relatives.

Sisters, this is only a suggestion of what Christ has done and is doing for womanhood. When the disciples came back from the city of Sychar to the well, where they had left their Master, they marvelled to find Him talking with a woman. In that day woman was low and vulgar. That a brilliant man, upon whose words the multitudes hung with breathless interest, should waste his time in intimate conversation with a working-woman, talking to her indeed as if she were his equal, caused great astonishment. But Jesus had no prejudices, no spirit of aristocracy; he recognized no social caste, except the divine one of brotherhood. I thank God that in our age, which has its black side, to be sure, there are yet many indications of the working of the leaven of Christian spirit in the common life of the people. Mr. Stopford Brooke has recently given a fascinating description of Tintoret's "Last Supper." It is a common room in which the apostles and the Master meet. Servants hurry to and fro; the evening has fallen dark, and the lamps are lit; those who eat the meal are really fishermen and unlearned men; here and there are incidents which prove that the artist wished to make us feel that it was just such a meal as was eaten that night by every one else in Jerusalem. We are indeed in the midst of common human life. But the upper air of the chamber is filled with a drift of cherubim; and the haze of the lamplight falls on and envelops the upright figure of the Christ, worn and beautiful, and bending down to offer to one of the disciples the broken bread. It is common human life, filled with the Divine.

I covet for you, young women, this pure and lofty fellowship, which shall glorify your common life, and take out of it all that is monotonous or prosaic. I pray for you, that you may rise to this holy ambition, — to be sisters of Jesus, in sympathetic service. Some of you remember, perhaps, the old legend, which relates how three ladies of high degree were once mentally exercised as to the relative fairness of their hands. The first had just passed her snowy fingers through the running stream, and pearl-like drops hung glittering from them. The second looked complacently at the rose tint derived from the strawberries she had culled. The third held fragrant flowers, and her hands were sweet with their breath. Up to this group came a needy woman, ragged and old, beseeching alms. Much disgusted at her appearance, they motioned her away; and she turned from them to a hardworking woman, whose toil-worn hands told of daily bread earned with difficulty. Then, as now, the poor were ready to help each other, even at the cost of self-denial. The workingwoman gave what she could from her scanty store; and the legendary beggar, transformed to an angel, was heard to say, "The most beautiful hands of all are those stretched out to consider and aid the poor."

The hands that bless the world most are the hands of sympathy which become the gentle messengers of a heart which, loving God with all its strength, loves its neighbor as itself.

Do not hesitate to follow any blessed impulse

toward helpfulness, because your capacity seems small or your opportunities trivial. A few years ago an invalid woman, whose home was in the country, visited a large city near which she lived, on a hot summer day. She had business in some of the smaller streets and alleys, and was appalled at the number of pale, puny, and sick babies in their mothers' arms, who were literally dying for a breath of fresh air. What could she do? "I cannot save all," she said, "but I may save one. There is room for a mother and her child at home." She took the one mother and her child out to her farmhouse, kept them for a fortnight, and then took them home and brought others. Some of her neighbors followed her example. The next summer the number of children entertained amounted to hundreds; the next, thousands.

Another woman, who lived in the city, and had neither money nor farmhouse, was sadly grieved that she could not help this most gracious charity. "I can at least tell others of it," she said. She wrote an account of it for a New York newspaper. A third woman, possessed of great wealth, on reading her article, sent a thousand dollars to the editor, with the request that he should open a fund for this noble purpose. The Fresh Air Charity was the result. The various organizations throughout the United

States for the removal of poor children from the poisonous air of the cities to the country, have grown out of this first attempt of a single half-sick farmer's wife to save one dying baby. If the woman who thought of it on that sultry day, as she passed sick and weary through the slums, had decided, "I cannot save all, why should I trouble myself with one?" how many lives that have been saved would have been lost!

There is nothing so contagious as a good action. Do promptly the generous deed toward which you are impelled, and God is able to multiply it and cause it to bring forth fruit an hundred-fold.

IV

CHRIST AND THE SICK

"I was sick, and ye visited me." — *Matt.* xxv. 36.
"And whithersoever he entered, into villages, or cities, or country, they laid the sick in the streets, and besought him that they might touch if it were but the border of his garment; and as many as touched him were made whole." — *Mark* vi. 56.

ORGANIZED care of the sick is, beyond question, the gift of Jesus Christ to mankind. Frederick W. Robertson puts it well when he says that, while Christianity did not create the feelings of tenderness and compassion, it did centralize them. To use his own words: "What Christianity did for all these feelings was exactly what the creation of the sun did for the light then existing. There was light before, but the creation of the sun was the gathering of all the scattered rays of light into one focus. Christian institutions, asylums, hospitals, are the reduction into form of the feelings that existed before."

Yet Christianity not only centralizes, but wonderfully develops as well, the capacity for sympathy and tenderness in the human heart.

The same writer I have quoted, in another

place compares the influence of Christianity to a mighty tropical river, which might pour its warm, fertilizing flood across the northern hemisphere, the result of which would be "the impartation of a vigorous and gigantic growth to the vegetation already in existence, and at the same time the development of life in seeds and germs, which had long lain latent in the soil, incapable of vegetation in the unkindly climate of their birth. Exactly in the same way, the flood of a divine life poured suddenly into the souls of men enlarged and ennobled qualities which had been used already, and, at the same time, *developed* powers which never could have become apparent in the cold, low temperature of natural life."

Lecky, the great historian of European morals, is responsible for the statement that the countless institutions of mercy which have covered the globe under Christianity were absolutely unknown to the pagan world. The ancient world was given over to selfishness.

Tacitus describes Rome of about the time of Jesus as a place of cruel rage, where the surest destruction came as "the consequence of virtues." Matthew Arnold sings of that time: —

> " On that hard pagan world disgust
> And secret loathing fell;
> Deep weariness and sated lust
> Made human life a hell.

In his cool hall, with haggard eyes,
The Roman noble lay;
He drove abroad in furious guise,
Along the Appian Way.

He made a feast, drank fierce and fast,
And crowned his hair with flowers —
No easier nor no quicker pass'd
The impracticable hours."

But in the midst of all this luxury there was not a single hospital for the sick. And in a later day, when the early Christians were endeavoring to follow the example of Jesus, and the Archdeacon Laurentius was called upon by the prefect of the city for the treasures of the early Roman Church, on his presenting under the colonnades the poor, the crippled, and the sick, whom he had sheltered and nourished, he was roasted alive as a punishment for his supposed sarcasm.

We have left to us a valuable store of Grecian literature, but in all its treasures there is no rich vein out of which grew, or might ever grow, an asylum for the sick and infirm. But Jesus, both by precept and example, turned the thought of mankind toward caring for the sick. The influence of Christianity could not be otherwise when we consider with how much dignity it crowns the individual human life. As one has said: " A crowded city, looked at merely as a mass of living beings, is no more dignified, and far more disgusting, than an ant-hill with its innumerable creeping lives. Looked on as a place in which each individual is a temple of the Holy Ghost, and every pang and joy of whom has in it something of infinitude, it becomes almost priceless in its value."

Once convince the world that human life is valuable, not because it is the life of a king or the life of some aristocrat, but because is the life of a man, the child of the infinite God, and you will naturally turn the inventive genius of the race toward caring for and protecting this precious treasure. This is exactly what Christianity did for mankind. It made the mind alert to discover and understand the beneficent secrets of nature. I suppose very few of us appreciate the priceless boon which God has granted to this generation in the diminution of pain. Over in the Public Garden there stands a statue in memory of one before whose wonderful discovery of anodynes all operative surgery was agonizing, after which it was painless. A great surgeon says: "Past all counting is the sum of happiness enjoyed by the millions who have in the last thirty-three years escaped the pain that was inevitable in surgical operations; pain made more terrible by apprehension, more keen by close attention; sometimes awful in a swift agony, sometimes prolonged beyond even the most patient endurance, and then renewed in memory, and terrible in dreams. This will never be felt again. And besides this abolition of pain, it would take long to tell how chloroform and ether have enlarged the field of useful surgery, making many things easy which were difficult, many safe which were perilous, many practicable which were nearly impossible."

Not only has Christianity made men alert to discover means of protecting and prolonging human life, but it has given men a new sense of responsibility, of our power to help each other. In a recent life of Dorothea Dix — which, by the way, I advise every young woman to secure and read as soon as possible — the story is told how, in her work for the insane, she became greatly impressed with the need of a new hospital for that purpose in the city of Providence. She told some of her friends that she intended to ask a very rich man, who had the reputation of being exceedingly miserly and utterly destitute of public spirit, to furnish the means.

Her friends assured her that her mission would certainly be futile; but she persevered in her determination, and called on this man in his home. He received her very coolly, and almost disdainfully asked her what she wanted. Her blood on fire, Dorothea Dix stood on her feet before him and stated her case. She told the astonished miser, as though it were a matter of the greatest possible personal interest and importance to him, of the sufferings and sorrows of these unfortunates. With flashing eyes she assured him that these wretched beings were his brothers and sisters, and that he could not escape the responsibility of his wealth and its power to help them. To this sordid soul, absorbed in money-getting, the terribly earnest appeal of this timid, but almost inspired, woman, was like a revelation from heaven. Its effect was very much like that when Jesus stood before Zaccheus, who, after a conversation with the Christ, said, "Lord, behold, half of my goods I give to the poor." The Providence miser looked up tremblingly into the face of Dorothea Dix, and said, humbly enough, "What do you want me to do?" "I want you," she said, "to give me fifty thousand dollars, to build additional quarters for these poor insane people." "I will do it," he said; and the victory was won. By no lever on earth could she have produced this result, except that which Christianity put in her hands.

In turning now to what the influence of Christianity is doing, in a public way, to heal the sick and care for the suffering in the city of Boston, I am embarrassed by a wealth of riches.

I can only glance at some of the great institutions that are an honor and a glory to our city.

First, there is our great City Hospital, with its spacious buildings that remind you of some European palace; with its splendid dome, which attracts the eye from every part of the city, second only in interest to the gilded dome on Beacon Hill, — one, the emblem of justice; the other, the emblem of mercy. Here is a notable staff of more than fifty physicians and surgeons, comprehending specialists in every department of medicine and surgery, with a large corps of trained nurses, skilled in the arts of kindness and sympathetic care.

And the marvel of it all is, that this palace, with its great array of learned and skilled physicians and trained attendants, is waiting, not to be of service to the rich and noble, to the aristocracy of the city, but specially to the poor and the unfortunate. Here is a wretched old tramp, hobbling along through some slum street in the North End. He is ragged and dirty. Surely nobody takes any care or interest in him, you say; but just now a careless driver in an express-wagon comes tearing around the corner, and, rushing into the narrow street, before the old man can get out of the way, he is thrown to the ground, and his arm is broken. What happens? A crowd of little boys and girls gather;

a few other wayfarers run to his assistance; a quick-witted boy, whose legs are as quick as his wit, hails the policeman on the next block; the policeman turns a key in the alarm-box on the corner; and in five minutes that poor old tramp, whom nobody seemed to care for before he was hurt, is being gently placed on a stretcher, lifted into the ambulance, and driven away to the City Hospital, where all the resources of the splendid institution are at his disposal. It is not so good a world as it ought to be, my brother, but do not forget that this is the only age in which the sun ever looked down on a scene of practical sympathy like that. There were treated last year in this hospital 6,502 patients, of whom 5,318 were healed. Besides these, there were treated outside of the hospital, in their own homes, but at the hospital's expense and care, 13,605 patients. After deducting all that was paid in return by people who were able to pay for their own treatment, the city expended, in this one superb charity alone, $168,641.11.

It would be like telling the same story over again, to recount the work of the Massachusetts General Hospital. Not far away from the City Hospital stands the Massachusetts Homœopathic Hospital, which, though in existence but a few years, is doing an excellent and philanthropic work.

CHRIST AND THE SICK 69

In South Boston our most attractive public building is the Carney Hospital, which cannot justly be overlooked in a summary of this kind. During the past three years it has received 3,124 patients, of which 2,674 were healed. Of these patients, 581 only paid in full, 609 paid in part, and 1,934 were both admitted and treated gratuitously. Besides these, 14,228 were treated as "out-patients." While this is a Roman Catholic institution, it is entirely non-sectarian in its treatment of patients and charitable service rendered. Quite a number of the members of this congregation were treated as "out-patients" during the last year; and at least one member of this church was admitted to the hospital, and for several weeks received as kindly and generous treatment as he could possibly have secured in an institution of our own.

At the corner of Ash and Bennett Streets is the headquarters of the Boston Dispensary, one of the most beneficent charities in the city, which has been growing in magnitude for ninety-four years. The Boston Dispensary signally illustrates the attitude of Christian civilization toward the sick. The wood-carving of the "Good Samaritan," which hangs in the lower hall, and the old picture of the same famous and blessed individual painted by John Johnson in 1797, also one of the heirlooms of the Dispensary, aptly indicate the spirit in which it was founded. The chief object of the Dispensary is to provide medical advice and medicines for the sick poor. There are in the central building on Bennett Street consulting rooms where fifteen physicians, all of them specialists, give their services free.

And if you will permit me to make the remark, I think it is only just to say that a wide observation leads me to the conclusion that no other class of men render so much service to the sick and suffering, without any anticipation of reward, as physicians.

Besides these office physicians, the Dispensary has the city divided into eleven districts. Each one of these districts is served by a resident physician, who receives a small salary paid by the Dispensary, so that his services are free to the patient. Three of these districts are in South Boston, which, with a single exception, receives more help from the Dispensary than any other district in the city.

The magnitude of the help rendered by this Dispensary was, I must confess, a great astonishment to me. During the first quarter of the year 1890, 14,541 patients were treated at the central office alone. During the second quarter, 16,209 were treated; and during the third quarter, ending with September last, 14,610. The last quarter of the year is not yet completed; but assuming the number of patients during that quarter to be equal to the third, 59,970 persons will have received medical relief and advice from the Dispensary during the year 1890. During the nine months 46,339 prescriptions have been filled.

Those who have work, and are able to do so, pay an average of ten cents for each prescription; but all who are unable to pay, receive medicine as well as treatment free. Besides these, the average number of prescriptions to outside patients amount to about 1,000 per month.

On the same street, standing next door to the Dispensary, is the South End Diet Kitchen, a wisely-conceived and most gracious charity. The purpose of this unique society, of which Mrs. P. C. Brooks is president, is to extend help to the poor in the discouraging and critical time of illness. When we consider how hard sickness is to bear, even when surrounded by delicate comforts, with kind friends searching the markets to find dainties to tempt our appetite and woo back our strength, we must in some feeble degree — and yet it is only a feeble degree — realize the suffering of those who have not the means to procure the nourishing food necessary to restore health and strength. Tickets are distributed by dispensary doctors, city missionaries, the Bible-readers, nurses, and Associated Charities' agents. These people, above all others, are brought into personal contact with the poor, and are in the best position to know the needs of the recipients. During last year there were dispensed to 13,194 families, 13,919 quarts of milk, 19,789 eggs, 2,540 pints of beef-tea and mutton-broth. How much of added comfort and happiness this timely assistance must have brought to anxious watchers who were otherwise unable to obtain this healthful nourishment for their sick! Another diet kitchen at the North End does a still larger work.

I am not attempting, of course, to give you even an outline of all the hospital work of the city; time would fail me to recount the good work done by the Massachusetts Lunatic Hospital, the New England Hospital for Women and Children, the Free Hospital for Women, the Murdock Hospital, St. Elizabeth's Hospital, and many other noble and worthy institutions which I have not space even to name. It is my province, rather, to give a free-hand sketch here and there which will show you something of the scope and the spirit of Boston Christianity's attitude toward the sick.

One of the sweetest charities of this kind,

working in relation to all the rest, and breathing upon each something of its own fragrance, is the Boston Flower and Fruit Mission. Everybody knows that flowers are acceptable to the sick; but the eagerness with which they are watched for at the hospitals, and up in dark, gloomy attics, is hard to realize, unless it comes within personal observation.

> "Only a blossom,
> Just the merest bit of bloom, —
> But it brings a glimpse of summer
> To the little, darkened room!"

This society interests the school-children in many towns about, who gather the wild flowers in the spring and summer, and send them in with a bit of paper on which is printed: "For the poor, sick little boys and girls in the hospital." Generous people throughout the country, who have large gardens, are also solicited for contributions, until many hundreds of baskets of beautiful flowers pass through their hands.

The diet kitchens, of which I was speaking only a moment ago, were supplied twice a week through last spring and summer with bouquets, which were dispensed with the milk and soup. I have no doubt that in many cases the bouquet is of as much value to the patient as the nourishment.

One of the ladies connected with the mission

says it may be a mere matter of sympathy and sentiment, but it is the one thing that brings a moment of brightness and joy into a sick-room. The iron bedsteads, the clean white beds, the polished, stainless floors, the white walls of a hospital, look clean, and fresh, and orderly, to a visitor. But to the patient who has stared at them, and been stared back at by them, for weeks and months, they look bloodless, cold, and severe. A bunch of fresh, fragrant flowers in a room like this brings a joy to the heart of the invalid, which none but that invalid can appreciate.

Another lady tells how she went one day last summer into a large tailoring shop in Boston, where some two hundred women and girls were at work. As she passed around with her basket of flowers, a quiet young girl came up to her and asked for "white ones, if you have them." Something in the voice startled the lady; and as she looked into the girl's sad face she noticed that her eyes filled with tears. "They are all lovely," she said, "but I only want a few white ones. Our baby died last night, and when I saw you come in I thought I would ask you for a few white ones for him; it will cheer his mother up a bit." God bless the Flower Mission, and all the people whose Christly spirit moves them to aid in its blessed work!

But let us not forget that, while Jesus was a great Physician of the body, his chief mission was to heal the sin-sick soul. And while Christianity is leavening every nation it touches with its own spirit of sympathy and tenderness toward the sick, its chief mission, like that of its divine Founder, is to bring healing to the diseased heart. Christ, and Christ alone, can

> "Minister to a mind diseased,
> Pluck from the memory a rooted sorrow,
> Raze out the written troubles of the brain,
> And with some sweet, oblivious antidote
> Cleanse the stuff'd bosom of that perilous stuff
> Which weighs upon the heart."

V

THE CHRISTIAN'S HORIZON

"Thou hast set my feet in a large room."—*Ps.* xxxi. 8.

MEN want room. It is one of the intuitions of our humanity. All history is full of illustrations. The American pioneers who pressed their way out from the settlements along the Atlantic coast, into the forests of Western Massachusetts and New York, were seeking after room. The next generation that climbed the Alleghanies, peopled the Ohio River valley, followed Daniel Boone into Kentucky, was obedient to the same instinct. The young men who a little later listened to Horace Greeley, and crossed the Mississippi River, and began the work of civilization on the great plains, were in the same line of succession. Fremont climbing the Rocky Mountains, Kennan or Schwatka or Greely clambering over the icebergs of the Arctics, Stanley crawling through the dense forests of the "darkest Africa," all tell the same story, and are indications of the same restless spirit and unsatisfied demand of the soul. In a physical way, Joaquin Miller gives voice to this feeling in his song of the "Inland Empire:"—

"Room! room to turn round in, to breathe and be free,
And to grow to be a giant, to sail as at sea,
With the speed of the wind — on a steed with his mane
To the wind, without pathway, or a route or a rein.
Room! room to be free, where the white bordered sea
Blows a kiss to a brother as boundless as he."

In a higher sense, the old Puritans were an illustration of this same spirit. Their whole history is the story of a struggle for room, — room to think — room to believe. This drove them from England to Holland, and from Holland to the sea. "They could not live by king-made creeds or rules."

Whittier, in his last poem, gives it as one of the chief attractions of the haven of eternal rest, that there —

"Every bark has sailing room."

It is our purpose this morning to show the grand office of our Christianity in satisfying this demand of humanity in the highest and noblest sense; to show that it broadens the horizon of our lives.

I.

Christianity enlarges the horizon of the intellect. It awakens men to the grand possibilities of human thought. One of the most brilliant thinkers of this country, who has made himself an honorable name throughout the civilized world by his power of sustained and lofty thinking, says of himself, that twenty-five years ago he was driving a hack, without any conception that he had a head worth using; but he was converted to Christ, and that spiritual regeneration proved to be a regeneration of mind as well. Perhaps no more apt illustration of the power of Christianity to enlarge and glorify the mental vision can be found, than in the history of art. The magnificent paintings that fill the art galleries of Italy had their birth in a revival of religion. Savonarola, St. Francis, and their heroic followers among the Italian monks of the Middle Ages, were the real founders of those splendid schools of art. The historian declares of Giotto that "he was no less remarkable as a Christian than as a painter."

The Florentine associations laid great stress on personal piety. The fraternities of painters held periodical meetings to render praise and thanksgiving to God. It was said of Fra Angelico that he never took up a pencil without first having recourse to prayer, and that whenever he painted a crucifixion the tears streamed down his face. The epitaph of this saintly artist expresses the spirit of the highest art of the fifteenth century: "To me be it no glory that I was a second Apelles, but that all my gains I laid at thy feet, O Jesu."

Michael Angelo's great themes, both in sculpture and painting, show that his genius was fired by the same mighty torch.

There is something in the splendid conception of humanity as set forth by Christianity, which gives breathing-room for the mind.

II.

It enlarges the horizon of the moral judgment. It gives a clearer, truer atmosphere in which to behold the relative values of temporal and spiritual things. Over on the Lake Shore Railroad in Ohio there lived a rich old German, a large grain dealer. One night his elevators took fire, and something like a quarter of a million dollars went up in flames. The next morning the old German, with his friends, stood about the smoking pile of black *débris*, looking gloomy enough.

In the midst of the blackened mass there was still a considerable quantity of grain, which, though badly damaged, was not entirely destroyed. A party of speculators came, and, after investigating a little, offered him fifteen thousand dollars for the pile. He had not dreamed of getting that much out of it, and accepted the offer gladly. As he was making out a bill of sale he overheard one of the men say to another, "What a grand lot of whiskey that will make!" The old man was on his feet in a moment. "What's that?" said he; "are you going to make whiskey out of that grain?" "Yes; why not?" "Well, then you don't." And he broke off the transaction right there. Some of his friends plead with him: "You are not in a position to be over-scrupulous; you have lost a quarter of a million dollars, you are not sure yet but you will turn out a bankrupt; and, after all, what does it matter to you what they do with your grain? You are not responsible for what becomes of it after it passes out of your hands." Then the grand old German straightened himself up and said, "Gentlemen, I know I have lost my elevators, and my hundreds of thousands of bushels of grain have gone up in smoke; but if you think my principles burned up last night with my wheat, then you are mistaken, that's all." That old German had clear eyes, and looked through a moral atmosphere that made it possible for him to weigh things at their true value.

There is a time coming when the wisdom of his decision will be manifest. Lowell, in his song of "America," sings of the Weighing Time; there —

> "Stood the tall archangel, weighing
> All man's dreaming, doing, saying,
> All the failure and the gain,
> All the triumph and the pain,
> In the unimagined years,
> Full of hopes, more full of tears,
> Since old Adam's conscious eyes
> Backward searched for Paradise,
> And, instead, the flame-blade saw
> Of inexorable law.
>
> In a dream I marked him there,
> With his fire-gold flickering hair,
> In his blinding armor stand,
> And the scales were in his hand;
> Mighty were they, and full well
> They could poise both heaven and hell.
> 'Angel,' asked I humbly then,
> 'Weighest thou the souls of men?
> That thine office is, I know.'
> 'Nay,' he answered me; 'not so,
> But I weigh the hopes of man
> Since the power of choice began
> In the world of good or ill.'
> Then I waited and was still.
>
> In one scale I saw him place
> All the glories of our race:
> Cups that lit Belshazzar's feast,
> Gems the wonder of the East,

Kublai's sceptre, Cæsar's sword,
Many a poet's golden word,
Many a skill of science, vain
To make men as gods again.

In the other scale he threw
Things regardless, outcast, few,
Martyr-ash, arena-sand,
Of St. Francis' cord a strand,
Beechen cups of men whose need
Fasted that the poor might feed,
Disillusions and despairs
Of young saints with grief-grayed hairs,
Broken hearts that break for man.

Marvel through my pulses ran,
Seeing then the beam divine
Swiftly on this hand decline,
While earth's splendor and renown
Mounted light as thistle-down."

III.

Christianity broadens the horizon of our sympathies. Christ came to make mankind one. Humanity was broken asunder: He came to bring it together in brotherhood. When the proud lawyer asked Jesus, "Who is my neighbor?" and Jesus told the story of the good Samaritan, it greatly shocked the prejudices of the people that heard Him. Christianity shows us that our neighbor is whoever needs us, and whom we can help.

A man who lives in Georgia, or Mexico, or Japan, may be more my neighbor than the man who lives next door to me. Florence Nightingale was a neighbor to the English soldiers in the Crimean War. William Lloyd Garrison was a neighbor to the slaves in Louisiana. When Charleston was shaken to pieces by an earthquake, Boston was her neighbor inside of twenty-four hours. When Jacksonville and Memphis were smitten with yellow fever, the gold-hunters of Idaho, the grape-growers of California, and the lumber-men of Puget Sound, alike recognized them as neighbors. That is the spirit of Christianity. The horizon lifts at its coming. It brings all mankind into one neighborhood. May God give us more and more of what some poet has described as —

> " A sense of an earnest will
>   To help the lowly-living,
>   And a terrible heart-thrill
>   When we have no power of giving.
>   An arm of aid to the weak,
>   A friendly hand to the friendless,
>   Kind words — so short to speak —
>   But whose echo is endless.
>   The world is wide, these things are small,
>   They may be nothing, but they are all."

A large part of the kingdom of Holland is many feet below high-water mark. One may stand inside the embankment and hear the heart-beat of the ocean far above his head. The surplus water on the surface of the country is pumped up by innumerable large windmills, and poured into the sea at low water by means of a system of canals. To accomplish this, engineers in all parts of the country are in constant telegraphic communication with a central office, from which, as from a brain, orders are sent to open the canal-locks here, and close them there, so as to keep the waters everywhere at the proper level. Without such a perfect system, Holland might be inundated at any time; but by this complex machinery, the inhabitants live safely below the level of the sea. So it is the purpose of our Christianity to make this whole world a safe and happy place to live in, by bringing men everywhere not only into sympathy with each other, but into friendly touch and communion with the loving heart of God, who, back of all combinations, is the great Combiner.

IV.

Christianity broadens the horizon of our activities. It exalts us by making us workers together with God. The humblest work becomes glorious if performed with a noble purpose, and in royal company. In the lower hall of the State House on Beacon Hill, where hang the treasures which Massachusetts soldiers brought back from many a bloody battle-field of the Rebellion, there is one pole from which the banner has been entirely torn away. That naked pole is not without its history.

It was carried at Fort Wagner, at the head of the colored soldiers from Massachusetts. The color-bearer was wounded, his flag was torn by shot and shell, but he crawled out through the agony of wounded and dying men, clasping his naked staff to his bosom, crying over and over again, "It did not touch the ground, it did not touch the ground!" He had caught the spirit of the heroic struggle in which he was engaged. So Christianity lifts us out of the mere struggle for bread. We still struggle for bread indeed, but the earthly loaf becomes an emblem of the bread which came down from heaven. Our little daily struggle against temptation and sin becomes a part of the great battle which Jesus is fighting for the redemption of this world. We keep pace with Jesus; we are carrying his banner; the spirit of his heroism is upon us; we are exalted and ennobled. How this enlarges the horizon of our life-work! Death is no longer the wreckage-place, where all life's cargo is scattered on the rocks. To the Christian, death is only the tide-rip where the river-current meets the sea. The poet sings : —

"Over ten thousand miles of pathless ocean
    The ship moves on its steadfast course each day;
  Through tropic calms, or seas in wild commotion,
    And anchors safe within the expected bay.

O ship of God! with voyage more sublime —
O human soul! In thine appointed hour,
Launched from eternity on seas of time,
In calms more fatal, storms of madder power, —

Sail on! and trust the compass in thy breast;
Trust the diviner heavens that round thee bend,
And, steering for the port of perfect rest,
Trust, most of all, in thine Eternal Friend."

VI

PETER AND HIS METHODS AT PENTECOST[1]

"Now when they heard this, they were pricked in their hearts, and said unto Peter and to the rest of the apostles, Men and brethren, what shall we do ? Then Peter said unto them, Repent, and be baptized every one of you, in the name of Jesus Christ, for the remission of sins, and ye shall receive the gift of the Holy Ghost." — *Acts* ii. 37, 38.

PENTECOST is a wonderful picture. How many workers for God, worn and weary in the battle against the unbelief and sin of their time, have gone back to Pentecost for courage, and have come away from studying anew its sharply drawn characters with new zeal and new strength!

It is an heroic picture. A little band of perhaps a hundred and twenty men and women on one side, and all the world on the other! History never tires us by repeating the story of the three hundred Lacedæmonians who withstood the army of invaders in the mountain-pass of old ; but here were less than half as many marshaled against the world, not simply to defend

[1] Delivered in a series of discourses on " Bible Revivalists." Published in *The Treasury*, July, 1890.

themselves, but inspired with the hope of universal conquest.

On one side was Jewish bigotry, cynical Grecian contempt, and the strong, hard hand of Roman hate. Over against these stood a little band of men and women, without arms, or culture, or social position, preaching a crucified Redeemer. They undertook this struggle, not in an age when freedom of speech was recognized, but at a time when the paw of a lion or the horn of a maddened bull was the ordinary answer of tyranny to the argument of an opponent.

History holds no more heroic picture. The central figure is Peter, bold to rashness, impulsive to a fault, but tender of heart; and when at last entirely subdued by the conquering love of Jesus, as true as the magnet to the steel in his undying love to the Redeemer. Peter's faults bring him close enough to us to make him helpful in our infirmities.

There are some triumphant epochs in his life that would discourage us, were it not that there is brought out in sharp outline the rough, rugged path he had to climb to reach them. But when we see him in his impulsive wilfulness refusing to let Jesus wash his feet, and then, a moment later, shamed by the Saviour's rebuke, exclaiming, "Not my feet only, but my hands and head also," we feel that he is one of us — our cheeks burn and redden with his shame. And how many of us have watched him as with strange fright and cowardice he denies the Lord in that outer court; and then, shivering, as though the mean lie had frozen the blood in his veins, he hovers down over the fire trying to warm his numb fingers; and then, at the tender, pained look of the patient Saviour, he goes out and weeps bitter tears of anguish. Ah, how many of us have gone out with him and wept the same tears that seemed to scorch our very souls!

Happy has it been for us if we have kept him company in his repentance, and have entered with him upon the new life of confidence and faith! How little Peter thought in the gray dawn of that cold morning, that there would ever be a Pentecost for him, when God would honor him as rarely, if ever, he had honored man before. There may be some one here to-night who needs just this word of encouragement. You have known the Lord, and he was kind to you as he was to Peter. You have denied him, and your heart bleeds to-night because you did it, and you fear to come back to his presence again. O my brother, let me preach to you the hopefulness of this rich gospel! Even from the dark background of sin and shame where you stand now, there is a Pentecost for you if, like Peter, you will repent of your sin, and return in humble obedience to your Saviour's service. And this leads me to the reflection that there is a most suggestive background to this entire picture of Pentecost. The background is "an upper room" where for days and weeks these men and women so heroic now had waited in deep humility and pleading before God — waited to be given spiritual power from on high. What tender days those must have been! Mary, the mother of Jesus, was there; and John, the beloved disciple, who had laid his head on Jesus' breast at the last supper; and Thomas, who had thrust his hand into the pierced side of Jesus before he could believe. They were waiting for power from on high before going out to proclaim the Word of him they loved so well. At last it came, — the spiritual baptism that John had foretold beside the Jordan, and Jesus had promised in that last sacred hour of separation. And lo! their timidity was gone, their fear of men, their fear of death; only their deep love for Jesus, and the importance of his message, possessed their souls: all else was insignificant. With throbbing hearts they went out to the conquest of the world. So, brothers and sisters, if we are to win great victories for our Lord, there must be a background of prayer. If we would have the multitude of perishing souls about us rescued from the thraldom of sin, we must pray as these heroic souls prayed before the first Pentecost.

"Such prayer would bring another Pentecost, and we need such a season to-day. We want the world to be evangelized; but we must remember that he who redeemed it, and commanded his apostles to evangelize it, forbade them to leave Jerusalem on their glorious mission till they were endued with power from on high. . . . There never was and never will be a substitute for this spiritual power, this holy anointing."

We are much better organized for our work than were these first Christian workers, but we must not depend too much upon our church machinery; for, after all, the church organization is only a cistern, useless enough unless it is full of the water of life. How ineffectual would be our great and expensive water system for the city of Boston, if Chestnut Hill reservoir were empty! So a church's machinery may be perfect, yet multitudes die at its very doors of spiritual thirst. The church must abound in spiritual life that comes only through the channel of prayerful consecration.

Out on the great sage-brush plains, where all

is parched and dry, men bore down hundreds and sometimes thousands of feet into the heart of the earth, until they come on streams of water that flow from mountain reservoirs far away out of sight, and living water bursts out in the desert and flows perpetually for the thirsty. The church ought to be an artesian well in the sin-burdened deserts of the world. The crying demand is for increased spiritual life in the church. Give us that, and the deadly grip of materialism will be thrown off, souls will be converted, revivals will spring up as naturally as flowers and foliage come in spring. Have you never watched how harmoniously and naturally the springtime comes? The sunshine imparts new life to the roots of the trees, and upwards, as blood bounds from the heart, new life is given to the branches, covering them with abundant leaf and flower. The birds catch the inspiration of this springtime revival; and from forest tree and orchard bough ten thousand robins and bobolinks and thrushes sing, — not because they ought to, but because they cannot help it. The necessity comes from the very joyousness of their hearts. So when the church gets close to God in daily communion, — at family altar, in secret closet, in pure, patient, cheerful life, — on such a church the Sun of Righteousness arises, the warmth of spiritual sunshine penetrates to the very roots of its life, and the conversion of sinners and rescuing of perishing men and women are the natural fruitage of its perpetual springtime glory.

The kind of preaching so effective on this historic occasion is also of the greatest suggestive value to us. It was Jesus, and the Cross, and the Resurrection; but it was the definite personal relation of the listening audience to these great truths, upon which Peter put the emphasis.

It was a very different sermon from that preached to Cornelius. When Peter preached to murderers, he left no doubt on their minds as to whom he meant. He might have preached on Corinthian impurity, or Roman idolatry, all day, and not made a single convert; but with splendid courage, and no less splendid common sense, he thundered in their trembling ears their own personal sin against the Christ they had taken "with wicked hands" and had "crucified and slain." No wonder they "were pricked in their hearts" when they heard that. Men are still pricked in their hearts when they hear that kind of preaching. Do you say they will not go to hear such preaching now? I answer, they cannot stay away from hearing it.

An empty thundering against sin in the abstract will empty the pews fast enough; but a heart-searching rebuke of the blood-red sins that scorch the souls of the men who listen, if given by a man who is in truth the messenger of Jesus, will not lack for hearers in this or any age; and the same response will come back now as to Peter, "Men and brethren, what shall we do?" We must preach to the consciences of men. Inspector Byrnes of New York says: "The great lieutenant of every police officer is that mysterious thing called conscience. You let a man try to deceive himself and lie to himself about himself, and that something comes knocking up against the shell of his body, and thumping on his ribs with every heart-beat, and pounding on his skull until his head aches, and he wishes he were dead, and groans in agony for relief. It is the same conscience that makes a criminal 'give himself away,' if one only knows how to awaken it, or stir it into activity. I never let a man know for what he is arrested. He may have committed a dozen more crimes of which I know nothing. If I lock him up alone, and leave him to the black walls and his guilty conscience for three or four hours, while he pictures the possible punishment due him for all his crimes, he comes presently into my hands like soft clay in the hands of the potter. Then he is likely to tell me much more than I ever suspected." So the conscience is the great lieutenant of every preacher of the Gospel. And this is not a lesson for the pulpit alone, for one of the most suggestive features of the Pentecost revival is that the church-members were all preachers that day. It was not Peter's sermon alone, but a hundred and twenty men and women in hand-to-hand, heart-to-heart conflict with the astonished multitude; and no doubt many who were converted in the forenoon were the most effective preachers among their old friends and associates in the afternoon. Ah! my brethren, give us the same conditions here, and Pentecost shall come to Dorchester Heights.

Finally, this picture ought to lead us to have courage to expect immediate results from the faithful preaching of the Gospel. One of the most dangerous errors that ever was propagated by the enemy of souls — an error that paralyzes the tongue of the preacher and the prayer of the church — is that Christianity is only a system of culture, and that souls are to be ransomed by gradual stages. Christianity does indeed cultivate souls. Civilization, with all its inventions and arts and comforts, attends Christianity wherever it prevails; but its first great work is to bring life to the dead.

You cannot cultivate until there is life. You might as consistently lay out a plan of education for a dead man as develop a scheme of spiritual culture for an unconverted sinner. Men and women are " dead in trespasses and in sins." What they need is spiritual resurrection — the spell of sin must be broken. The heart with its love of bad things must be cleansed so that it will love the good and abhor the evil.

That work God did at once for the repenting sinners at Pentecost; and, glory be to his name, he has lost neither his willingness nor his power!

VII

OUR SISTER PHŒBE, THE DEACONESS

"I commend unto you Phœbe our sister, who is a deaconess of the church that is at Cenchreæ; that ye receive her in the Lord, worthily of the saints, and that ye assist her in whatsoever matter she may have need of you; for she herself also hath been a succourer of many, and of mine own self." — *Rom.* xvi. 1 (*Revised Version, marginal reading*).

WE have to go into the margin here to find the word deaconess; in the text it is rendered servant. It is one of the strange illustrations of the power of prejudice and conservatism on really good men. For if this same word had been used to describe the church office of a man, it would have been translated deacon, as it is in many other places in the New Testament; but because it touches the vexed question of a woman's right to official relation to the church, it was impossible to bring the word deaconess nearer than the margin.

Nevertheless, it is sure that the order of deaconesses made its mark so plainly on the track of early church history that it has been impossible for its footprints to be entirely obliterated. We make no claim for the deaconess movement that it is anything new in the religious world, but rather, as Frances Willard aptly puts it, a revival of one of "the lost arts," more important than any that used to fire the eloquence of Wendell Phillips.

The occasion of this commendation of Phœbe by the Apostle Paul was her visit to Rome, probably on official business for the church, and quite possibly to carry this very letter to the Romans, in which she is so generously commended. The description that is given of Phœbe and the character of her work, as well as the references made to the official service of other women in the early church, very clearly mark the distinction between the order of deaconesses and the nuns or sisterhoods of the Roman Catholic Church. Dr. De Sanctis, who for many years occupied a high official position at Rome, describes three classes who take the veil as nuns: " First, young girls who become interested in religion, and, blindly following the path of piety, believe the priest's declarations against conjugal love and domestic affection as unholy, and tending to eradicate the love of Christ. Second, those who, failing to captivate the regard of men, are yet conscious of an irresistible need of loving some object, and therefore seek to be loved, as they say, by the Lord Jesus Christ, who is represented as a young man of marvelous beauty and most winning look, with a heart shining with love, and seen transparent in his breast. Third, those who, being educated from childhood in the nunnery, remain there and become nuns without knowing why, and give up with alacrity a world which they have never seen." The order of deaconesses is now, and always was, something entirely different from this. Canon Sumner well says: "It is surely a mistake to suppose that nuns and deaconesses are synonymous terms. Convents are ostensibly houses for the sheltering of those who think that they can serve God better by retiring from the world for the purposes of meditation and prayer. Deaconess institutions are for those women who desire, in a stated, formal, and authorized manner, to be set apart for active work in the church of God. The two are wide as the poles apart."

I have detained you at considerable length with this point because I fear that the revival of the deaconess movement has awakened a fear in the minds of some that we were launching on the religious seas a species of Protestant nunnery. This is not so. The deaconess was in early times, and is to be to-day, selected from the mature women of the church, whose special gifts and graces indicate their usefulness as helpers in that office, just as a steward or class-leader or Sunday-school superintendent is selected. She is placed under no vow, but is free to act under the impulse of the Spirit of Christ, who reigns in the heart. The founder of the Paris Deaconess Institute says: "No vows, no poverty, no monastic obedience. We took as the ground of our efforts not the pretence of salvation by works, but the duty of witnessing by works our love to Him who came down from heaven to save us."

It seems strange that such an institution should ever have been permitted to die out of the religious world. It can only be explained by studying the growth of monachism in the church. It is interesting to note that in the last three hundred years every revival of spirituality in the church has been marked by an increased liberality toward woman, and an effort to utilize her as a practical force in church work.

We may see this in Holland in the years just before the Puritan fire burned its way across the Atlantic to Plymouth Rock. Gov. Bradford gives this quaint picture of a good Dutch deaconess in Amsterdam in 1606: —

"She honored her place, and was an ornament to the congregation. She usually sat in a convenient place in the congregation, with a little birchen rod in her hand, and kept the children in great awe from disturbing the congregation. She did frequently visit the sick and weak, especially women, and, as there was need, called out maids and young women to watch and to do them other helps as their necessity did require; and if they were poor, she would gather relief for them of those that were able, or acquaint the deacons; and she was obeyed as a mother in Israel, and an officer in Christ."

No doubt the inferior social position of women at this time was sufficient to make abortive the attempt to re-establish the order of deaconesses permanently among our Puritan fathers and mothers.

I have only time to glance for a moment at the most wonderful modern development of the deaconess movement in Germany, and yet it, too, was the outcome of a spiritual awakening. A young German pastor named Fliedner goes over to England and meets Elizabeth Fry, and wanders on to Scotland and meets Thomas Chalmers, and in contact with these great souls his heart is lighted with a holier fire. From beside Dr. Chalmers he writes home: "The Lord greatly quickens me." Now when a man is genuinely quickened in soul by the Lord, it always gets into his hands and feet. It is ever as it was with Peter on the housetop. His heavenly vision is only a preparation for the messenger who says, "Three men seek thee;" and the quickening of that revelation from God is soon being put into the fleet steps that carry him toward the house of Cornelius.

Fliedner was no exception. He had scarcely reached his home in Kaiserwerth, before a poor woman, a discharged convict, knocked at his door for sympathy and help. Fliedner and his noble wife fitted up their garden-house, twelve feet square, for her; but the winds were only too glad to carry news like that, and others came; then a good girl from Fliedner's church started a knitting-school, and on it went.

That little garden-house, twelve feet square, has grown into a marvelous institution indeed, — a great system of reformatories, hospitals and schools. The first deaconesses were from these reformed women, who, having been ransomed by the devotion of others, consecrated their redeemed lives to the same blessed work. To-day there is a splendid system of institutions in Kaiserwerth with an income of a million dollars a year, with more than a score of affiliated houses in Germany, Italy, England, Asia Minor, Syria, and Northern Africa.

In Germany was witnessed the first Methodist venture in this direction; and although German society and government have presented in many ways a very unfriendly front to Methodism, yet these Methodist deaconesses have so won the hearts of the public that free steam and street car accommodations are granted them. The "forward movement" among the Wesleyans in England, the impulse of which is carrying on the grand work of the West Central Mission in London under the direction of Mark Guy Pearse and Hugh Price Hughes, two as heroic and dauntless spirits as Methodism has ever produced, has as one of its marked characteristics the revival of the deaconess. They call them the "Sisters of the People," but their service is identical with the deaconess of the early church and of Methodism in America.

It seems strange that Methodism should have delayed so long the re-establishment of this office. Liberality in the treatment of women in the work of the church was a part of our inheritance from Susanna Wesley, who has been well styled "the Mother of Methodism." Once during the long absence of her husband she opened the doors of the rectory for public worship, which she conducted herself. She read sermons, prayed, and talked persuasively to the people who thronged her home. The curate and the conservatives were greatly shocked, and appealed to her husband to stop it. In self-defence she says: —

"I chose the best and most awakening sermons we had. Last Sunday I believe we had about two hundred hearers, and yet many went away for want of room."

One can see here the germ of woman's freedom in the Methodist class-meeting and lovefeast, which has developed through the Sunday-school and the Woman's Home and the Woman's Foreign Missionary Societies.

And now that this deaconess plant is taking such a firm root in our congenial soil, we may really hope that Methodism is going to take Florence Nightingale's advice, and in the near future keep clear of all jargons about man's work and woman's work, and go her way straight to God's work in simplicity and singleness of heart, each one doing with all the might what each one can do best.

The mission of the deaconess and the character of her work cannot be better set forth than in these words of Paul, in our text, in commendation of Phœbe. The church is urged to be careful of her, because "she herself also hath been a succourer of many." She is to be peculiarly the church's hand of succor held out to those who are pursued by trials and sorrows.

The need of the church at the present hour, in grappling with the new problems of our great and our rapidly growing cities, no doubt explains the rapidity with which Methodist Deaconess Homes have sprung up in Chicago, New York, Cincinnati, Minneapolis, Detroit, Philadelphia, St. Louis, Buffalo, Cleveland, and Boston, and the interest which is becoming more earnest throughout the whole church.

Feeling the need of a closer bond of sympathy between the church and the homes of the common people, we hopefully and prayerfully say to the deaconess what Mordecai said to Esther: " Who knoweth whether thou art come to the kingdom for such a time as this?" The fields are white for the harvest.

How many homesick, lonely ones there are in this great city, who might be sought out and rescued from peril by such consecrated women! There are thousands of young men and young women in this city whose home-life has been left behind in the farmhouses and village cottages of these New England States. "All the rivers run into the sea," and the modern city is like the sea. All New England and the Provinces beyond are skimmed every year to supply Boston's demand for business energy; and of these thousands of young people, most of them were reared in Christian homes, and many of them consecrated to God in their childhood. But the temptations of the city are luring them away from the church. We must win them back to the old home fireside.

A young French soldier lay as if dying in a hospital in Geneva. They wrote to his father far away in Brittany, and as soon as possible the old white-haired sire of seventy years stood beside him. "You must not die!" cried the old man. But the youth protested that nothing could tempt his appetite, and the doctors had given him over to die. Then the old father took from his knapsack one of the common loaves of rye bread, such as are eaten by the peasants of Brittany. "Here, my son, take this; it was made by your mother."

The sick lad turned his heavy eyes, and, stretching out his hand greedily, cried, "Give it me, father; I am hungry!" As he ate, his eye lighted up, the blood came back to his face, and large tears rolled down his cheeks as he said, "It's so good, so good! the bread from my home!" From that hour the soldier began to get well. So I believe the deaconess is to help us hunt out these homesick hearts, and bring them a taste of bread from the old home. And no one who has had experience in hunting out the lost families in the crowded portions of the city will doubt for a moment the possibilities for great usefulness for the deaconess in seeking out and interesting the children in the Sunday-school and the church.

I was very much touched last year by a story in the report of the West Central Mission in London, of a playground extemporized out of the schoolroom under one of the mission halls. The Sisters of the People found that the children in the neighborhood knew no games, partly because they had no place to play, except in the busy streets. They therefore opened the schoolroom three afternoons a week, providing swings, skipping-ropes, and instruction in old-fashioned English games. It was a capital idea — at least so the children thought. The lady who tells the story says: "The swings are the greatest attraction, and many are the entreaties, 'Swing me higher, sister, higher!'"

As I read that, I thought how in another sense the children of these great cities are unconsciously crying, "Swing me higher, sister, higher!"

To the Christian Church this cry is ceaselessly coming. From cramped and dreary homes, from dirty and over-crowded attics, from drunken and brawling alleys, above the roar of ruthless traffic, from sick-beds and broken hearts, the cry comes evermore, "O bride of Jesus, sister of all the little ones for whom he died, swing me higher, still higher! into a purer air, where I may feel the 'joy of power' above the mud and fog, nearer to heaven, nearer to God!"

To all who love the Lord Jesus Christ, and long to see his triumph in the earth, — in the words of Paul with which we began, and having in mind all the noble women who shall present themselves for this blessed work, — "I commend unto you Phœbe our sister, who is a deaconess of the church."

VIII

SPIRITUAL NATURALIZATION

"Giving thanks unto the Father which hath made us meet to be partakers of the inheritance of the saints of light; who hath delivered us from the power of darkness, and hath translated us into the kingdom of his dear Son." — *Col.* i. 12, 13.

THE Bible picture of human life is full of dramatic power. It is that of an intelligent, hoping, aspiring, deathless soul, either struggling with spiritual enemies mighty in power and terrible in malignity, or held in the grasp of these evil forces a helpless slave. An immortal spirit winged with faith and hope, lured upward by white-winged seraphs, or tempted downward by dark demons from the pit.

There is an old picture of a scene in ancient Babylon. It is the "Chariot Race." It is a strange scene. There are chariots of brass, chariots of silver, chariots of iron, chariots of gold, all in one mad rush for the mastery. Excited, half-crazed charioteers lean forward in their chariots and lash the already frenzied steeds to a still wilder pace. Here and there is a broken chariot, a fallen steed, an overthrown driver crushed, bleeding, and dying, in the dust and *débris* of the wild arena. But the charioteers pay no heed to these, but rush by with the speed of the wind and the awful frenzy of the demon.

There is in this some suggestion of the Bible picture of human life. Immortal, never-dying souls, full of hope, full of ambition, in their chariots — some of brass, some of silver, some of iron, some of gold — are making the one breathless race of life from the cradle to the grave. And to add intensity to the picture, the curtain is drawn aside, and we are permitted to see that the whole spiritual universe is interested in, and taking part in, this whirling, rushing tide of human souls. That which we see outwardly of race and struggle is only a faint picture of the inward conflict that is going on in the great heart of humanity.

The critical passages of a man's life are not the outward happenings, but the inward, invisible, unjournalized, unspoken experiences through which the heart passes. Victor Hugo, in drawing his greatest character in fiction, Jean Valjean, says: "There is a spectacle grander than the sky, it is the interior of the soul. Conscience," he declares, "is the chaos of chimeras, envies, and attempts, the furnace of dreams, the lurking place of ideas we are ashamed of; it is the pandemonium of sophistry, the battle-field of the passions. At certain hours look through the livid face of a reflecting man; look into his soul, peer into the darkness. Beneath the external silence, combats of giants are going on there, such as we read of in Homer; *mêlées* of dragons and hydras, and clouds of phantoms such as we find in Milton. A glorious thing is the infinitude which every man bears within him, and by which he desperately measures the volitions of his brain and the actions of his life." Paul paints the same picture with a few simple but skilful touches when he says to the Ephesians: "Put on the whole armor of God, that ye may be able to stand against the wiles of the devil; for we wrestle not against flesh and blood, but against principalities, against powers, against the rulers of the darkness of this world, against spiritual wickedness in high places." The Bible picture we have before us is like this, and comprehends the epochs of that race from the deliverance of the soul by the grace of God out of the grip of the power of darkness, on to that final epoch of the good man's history when he shall enter into the inheritance of the saints in *light*. It begins in darkness, and ends in fadeless light. We have first a memorable deliverance.

"Who hath delivered us from the power of darkness."

There can be no doubt but that the plain, simple teaching of the Bible is that the world, the flesh, and the devil, with all their troop of passions, appetites, and habits, bind the natural man in chains of bondage. It is not taught that men and women are as wicked as they might be, or as they may become; but it is taught that the only way of salvation for any human soul lies in divine deliverance from the grasp of the power of darkness.

There is no other door into the fold of Christ except that one of entire cleansing from sin. If the butcher have a tainted spot in his quarter of beef, the only possible chance to save that which is good, even with the strongest preservatives, is the sharp knife that cuts out that which is already spoiled. So we are taught that sin is not a salvable article in God's universe, — it must be utterly separated from it. It is not enough that we simply cease to sin, and begin in the future to do well; we must be cleansed from the sins of the past, we must be delivered from the *power of darkness.*

David tried that method of simply keeping silent about his past sins; he tried, as many do to-day, to simply hush up and cover up his sins. *I kept silence*, he says. But underneath that silence his very bones roared. He could not get rid of sin by simply keeping silent; there it was in all its nakedness, standing out glaring in the light of God. "Memories met him and whispered in his ear, faces rose up and came near, and, looking at him, dumbly clamored against him. Fingers pointed at him. Nature seemed allied with conscience, and as he passed there came strange voices, looks, hints, whispers, evil omens, as if all the world knew all about it and shrank from this dreadful man. Above him was a God whom he feared to face. Beneath him was a blackness which he shuddered to think of, for in every man's heart sin means hell — it can mean nothing else."

You remember that weird and tragic story of Bulwer Lytton's, in which he tells of the murderer who tried to bury his crime. But the black pool would not hide his secret, and there, in the dried-up river-bed, lay the victim. He hid the accusing body in the forest, but the winds swept away the leaves and flung him again into sight. We have no power in ourselves to undo the past. We cannot hush it up. Its voices go on and on forever clamoring against us. We cannot bury it. It rises and pursues us. Francis I., King of France, stood counseling with his officers how he could take his army into Italy, when Ameril, the fool of the court, leaped out from a corner of the room and said, "You had better be consulting how you will get your army back;" and it was found that Francis I., and not Ameril, was the fool. Instead of consulting of the best way of getting into sin, men would better consult as to whether they will be able to get out of it.

The Gospel comes to deliver men from the power of darkness. We have as the result of this deliverance a translation, or naturalization, into an honorable citizenship. Paul says, "Translated us into the kingdom of his dear Son." This word "translated" is very significant. It means an absolute removal into another condition or sphere. It is the word used in relation to Enoch, who was carried up to heaven without passing through the gateway of death. So being delivered from the power of darkness, the soul is consciously translated, — removed into another spiritual kingdom. And I think the atmosphere of this age, more than any age in the past, is in sympathy with this doctrine of a conscious spiritual knowledge of the whereabouts of the soul. The great mass of Christian believers in this age have come to believe that, as Mrs. Willing says, "they may know whether they are to spend eternity wailing with devils or shouting with angels. Their salvation is not a mere numerical chance in a divine lottery, but according to law based upon character, which means volition, freedom of choice. They are no longer to gage their piety by ceaseless wadings through dismal swamps of doubt, their most helpful symptom a perpetual moan, —

> 'Do I love the Lord, or no?
> Am I His, or am I not?'

But even the little children may know of a surety that they have passed from death unto life."

And, my brethren, it is dignified and noble citizenship into which we have been translated. St. Paul, the writer of our text, himself considered it high honor that he was a Roman citizen. Yet how much more dignity and power and honor have accrued to Paul through his citizenship in the kingdom of Jesus! His Roman citizenship, proud as it was, did not save him from stripes and imprisonment, and finally an ignominious death. But if you were in the city of Rome to-day, and would walk down the Corso, there in the Piazza Colonna you might see a column a hundred and sixty-eight feet high that was originally built to commemorate the victories won by Marcus Aurelius in the Marcomannic wars. The imperial statue once surmounted it, but it was taken down by Sextus V., and a statue of St. Paul ten feet high was put in its place. How significant is that monument of St. Paul on the summit of the imperial pillar!

The poor prisoner, persecuted, despised, beheaded, is exalted to glory and honor, surmounting the memorials of the old Roman emperor's victories. It indicates the triumph of Christianity over Paganism, the dethronement of a proud imperialism by the power of the cross. It bears witness to the moral power of the Gospel, as incomparably superior to the military power of Rome. The latter expired fifteen centuries ago; the former still lives, " the power of God unto salvation to every one that believeth." So far from growing old, it is always renewing its youth. It never had so wide an influence in this world as at this moment. Let us not fail to appreciate the dignity of this heavenly citizenship.

When I come to you with the Gospel of Jesus, I am calling you to a higher, nobler, more honorable station than you have ever known.

You have been toiling hard and struggling for earthly positions that, after all, are only temporary and shadowy in possession. For the last few months we have seen great multitudes of men, prominent citizens, struggling for official appointments. If sinners were as anxious to get spiritual admittance and exaltation in the kingdom of heaven as some men are to secure office for themselves or friends, the kingdom of heaven would suffer violence, and the violent would take it by force. Oh, let me call you all this morning to the lofty stations awaiting you in the spiritual kingdom!

But the best of it all is, that this deliverance and new citizenship shall end in a glorious inheritance. " Which hath made us meet to be partakers of the inheritance of the saints in light."

After a while, blessed be God, we shall go home, and in the great court of the universe, and with him who spake as never man spake as our voluntary attorney to plead our cause, we will claim our inheritance. Some years ago an Englishman of a noble family became dissipated, went to sea, became a wanderer on the face of the earth, and, after drifting about all over the world, he was finally landed penniless in San Francisco. There he lived on the streets for years, from hand to mouth. One day a letter came bidding him come home and claim a great estate, and in the letter was a draft for a thousand pounds to come home on. What did he do? He went to the barber-shop and took a bath; his hair was trimmed, his unkempt beard was shaved, his rags went to the ragman, and he was dressed like a gentleman; and he who had been but a poor tramp on the face of the earth, crossed the continent in a drawing-room car, and hurried over the sea to claim his mansion So to the poor, wandering sons of God, degenerated by sin and a wicked life, God sends, bidding them get ready to come home, and knowing, as the English solicitor did, how bankrupt we are, he sends spiritual wealth enough to cleanse us and clothe us, and lend dignity and cheer to our faces, so that we may not creep home like ragged tramps, but come home like sons to the father's house.

And when we are ready he calls us across the seas to claim the mansion that is being prepared for us. Just what that blessed inheritance shall be, we may not know, but the most precious things of the universe are used in God's Word to make its glories known to us.

All resources are in his hand. He planted the gold in the mountains and the silver in the rocks. He buried the diamonds in the depths of the earth. He formed the pearls in the sea. All resources are his, all love is in his heart, all beauty is in his mind.

IX

THE SOURCES OF AMERICAN NATIONAL LIFE

A THANKSGIVING SERMON

"Have we not taken to us horns by our own strength?"
— *Amos* vi. 13.
"Blessed is the nation whose God is the Lord." — *Ps.* xxxiii. 12.
"He hath not dealt so with any nation." — *Ps.* cxlvii. 20.

STANDING at Gettysburg, one of the greatest battle-fields of the Republic, a place hallowed by the blood of thousands of American heroes, Senator Ingalls of Kansas made this remarkable statement in a public address: —

"The purification of politics is an iridescent dream. Government is force. Politics is a battle for supremacy. Parties are the armies. The Decalogue and the Golden Rule have no place in a political campaign. The object is success. To defeat the antagonist and expel the party in power is the purpose. In war it is lawful to deceive the adversary, to hire Hessians, to purchase mercenaries, to mutilate, to kill, to destroy. The commander who lost a battle through the activity of his moral nature would be the derision and jest of history. This modern cant about the corruption of politics is fatiguing in the extreme. It proceeds from the tea-custard and syllabub dilettanteism, the frivolous and desultory sentimentalism of epicenes."

Surely Christian men, without regard to politics, may be pardoned for uniting in thanksgiving that a man capable of uttering such sentiments bids fair to fail of re-election to the United States Senate. And yet, he is doubtless a representative of far too large a class of American citizenship, who look upon our national heritage as the product of American shrewdness or American luck. It has occurred to me, that, in connection with our national Thanksgiving week, it might be of profit to us all, and of special interest to the young, to carefully trace the streams of life and influence which united in the formation of our national character. America has a moral history, all her own, which is very unique. Dr. Gray of the *Interior* well says: " It is utterly impossible to tell the story of American history while ignoring the element of religion. The only common bond which runs through the biographies of American explorers, pioneers, and founders of States, is the thread of a Christian faith, the power of a religious purpose."

It is impossible to read the history of Christopher Columbus, human and faulty as he was in many respects, without being impressed with the deep religious sentiment which made all his enterprises grand and solemn to himself. When he set sail on his first voyage across the ocean, he wrote in his journal, which he kept for the inspection of the Spanish sovereigns: "Therefore your highnesses, as Catholic Christians and princes, lovers and promoters of the holy Christian faith, and enemies of the sect of Mahomet, and of all idolatries and heresies, determined to send me, Christopher Columbus, to the said parts of India, to the said princes and people and lands, and discover the nature and disposition of them all, and the means to be taken for the conversion of them to our holy faith." And when at last the weary voyage was over, and on that eventful Friday morning in October he first beheld the New World, each boat that carried himself and his officers to the land carried the standard of the cross; and when his feet touched the new land, he threw himself on his knees, kissed the earth, and returned thanks to God, with tears of joy. On his return home from the voyage, in the midst of a fearful storm at midnight, the officers and crew called on the aid of heaven. According to the superstitious customs of their time, a lot was cast for the performance of a barefooted pilgrimage to the shrine of Santa Maria de la Cueva in Huelva, and the lot fell upon Columbus. The historian, Las Casas, devoutly considered this an intimation from the Deity to Columbus that the fearful storm was all on his account, to humble his pride and prevent his arrogating to himself the glory of a discovery which was the work of God, and for which he had merely been chosen as an instrument.

I call your attention to this incident that you may see how universally the religious element entered into the thoughts of the people concerning the discovery of the New World. When Columbus finally landed at Palos, on his return, the bells were rung, the shops shut, all business suspended, and a grand procession was formed and marched through the streets to the principal church, to return thanks to God. The same religious spirit prevailed at the court of Spain when Columbus made his report to the sovereigns. In the presence of a great multitude he gave an account of the most striking events of his voyage and a description of the islands discovered. He displayed specimens of unknown birds and animals; of rare plants of medicinal and aromatic virtues; of native gold, in dust, in crude masses, or labored into barbaric ornaments; and, above all, the natives of these countries, who were objects of intense and inexhaustible interest. All these he pronounced mere harbingers of greater discoveries yet to be made, which would add realms of incalculable wealth to the dominions of Spain, and whole nations of proselytes to the true faith. At the

SOURCES OF AMERICAN NATIONAL LIFE 123

close of his address, the king and queen, and the brilliant crowd of notable persons present, sank on their knees, and raising their clasped hands to heaven, their eyes filled with tears of joy and gratitude, poured forth thanks and praises to God for so great a providence. The historian says : —

"A deep and solemn enthusiasm pervaded that splendid assembly, and prevented all common acclamations of triumph. The anthem, Te Deum Laudamus, chanted by the choir of the royal chapel, with the accompaniments of instruments, rose in full body of sacred harmony; bearing up, as it were, the feelings and thoughts of the auditors to heaven, so that it seemed as if in that hour they communicated with celestial delights."

Such was the solemn and pious manner in which the brilliant court of Spain celebrated this sublime event — offering up a grateful tribute of melody and praise, and giving glory to God for the discovery of another world. Washington Irving, to whose Life of Columbus I am indebted for these facts, declares that the great discoverer considered himself selected of Heaven as an agent; that his mind was elevated above selfish and mercenary views, and was filled with the same devout and heroic schemes which, in the time of the Crusades, inflamed the thoughts and directed the enterprises of the bravest warriors and most illustrious princes. The first gold which the New World yielded to the Old gilds the ceiling of one of the noblest churches of Rome. Genoa reverently preserves the sketch in which the great discoverer, by his own pencil, commemorated his success; representing himself as the servant of God, attended by Providence, and followed by Religion.

The early French discoverers were animated by the same spirit. The first colonies planted in Florida by the French were of the Huguenots. The northern discoveries of New France, which was destined to become New England, were pursued not wholly nor mostly for adventure or wealth, but because devout French Catholics desired to requite the Church for her losses through the tremendous influences of Luther and Calvin in the Old World, by winning to her fold the natives of the New. Cartier, La Roche, Champlain, and De Monts, were only the stormy petrels of this great religious movement. The French discoverers that pressed onward around Lake Huron, discovering the Mississippi River and pursuing it south to the Gulf, were all animated by the same religious spirit. It does not matter whether you praise or blame them, you cannot read history without respecting their earnestness and finding yourself convinced that it was a genuine religious enthusiasm that furnished the courage, the self-sacrifice, and the sublime endurance necessary to carry them through. The early English discoverers were of the same spirit and of a still nobler mould. Sir Humphrey Gilbert, who lost his life on the return voyage from this country, shouted as his last message to his fellow voyagers in a companion vessel, "We are as near to heaven by sea as by land." The heroic Sir Walter Raleigh, a step-brother of Gilbert, took up his work, and left his mark forever on the New World in the State of Virginia and the Carolinas. The religious idea stands out prominent in the records left to us of Virginia's colonization; we read of the faithful Indian chief, Manteo, receiving Christian baptism "by the commandment of Sir Walter Raleigh," and investing him with the rank of feudal baron as Lord of Roanoke.

The whole world knows how completely religion dominated the life and character of the Pilgrims. George Bancroft says: "Every enterprise of the Pilgrims began from God." Seldom have wiser or more reverent words been uttered than those of the Puritan Robinson, spoken in farewell to the Pilgrims who sailed on the Mayflower: —

"I charge you," said he, "before God and his blessed angels, that you follow me no further than you have seen me follow the Lord Jesus Christ. The Lord has more truth yet to break forth out of his holy Word. I cannot sufficiently bewail the condition of the reformed churches, who are come to a period in religion, and will go at present no further than the instruments of their reformation. Luther and Calvin were great and shining lights in their time, yet they penetrated not into the whole counsel of God. I beseech you, remember it — 'tis an article of your church covenant — that you be ready to receive whatever truth shall be made known to you from the written Word of God."

Edward Winslow, one of the Pilgrim voyagers, writes: —

"When the ship was ready to carry us away, the brethren that stayed at Leyden, having again solemnly sought the Lord with us and for us, feasted us that were to go, at our pastor's house, being large; where we refreshed ourselves, after tears, with singing of psalms, making joyful melody in our hearts, as well as with the voice, there being many of the congregation very expert in music; and indeed it was the sweetest melody that ever mine ears heard. After this they accompanied us to Delft-Haven, where we went to embark, and then feasted us again; and after prayer performed by our pastor, when a flood of tears was poured out, they accompanied us to the ship, but were not able to speak one to another, for the abundance of sorrow to part. And so, lifting up our hands to each other, and our hearts for each other to the Lord our God, we departed."

When, after a long and boisterous voyage of sixty-three days, they found themselves safely moored in the harbor of Cape Cod, even before they landed they formed themselves into a body politic, by signing a solemn compact, in which they declare that they undertake to plant the colony "for the glory of God and advancement of the Christian faith."

Such was the quality and spirit of the men who laid the foundations of state and national life in Massachusetts. One will search in vain in the life of these people for the exhibition of a spirit like that manifested by Senator Ingalls. They did not believe that they had taken unto themselves horns by their own strength. Governor Bradford, who was the first governor selected in the New World, has left a fragmentary poem on New England, in which he sings,—

> " Famine once we had,
> But other things God gave us in full store,
> As fish and ground-nuts, to supply our strait,
> That we might learn on Providence to wait;
> And know, by bread man lives not in his need,
> But by each word that doth from God proceed.
> But awhile after plenty did come in,
> From His hand only who doth pardon sin.
> And all did flourish like the pleasant green,
> Which in the joyful spring is to be seen."

William Tappan describes the early Thanksgiving days among these New England colonists. He says : —

> " When the old fathers of New England sought to
> Honor the heavens with substance and with first-fruits,
> They with their blessings — all uncounted — summed up
> 　　　Their undeservings.
>
> They praised Jehovah for the wheat sheaves gathered;
> For corn and cattle, and the thrifty orchards;
> Blessings of basket, storehouse, homestead, hamlet;
> 　　　Of land and water.

> They praised Jehovah for the depth of riches
> Opened and lavished to a world of penury;
> Mines, whose red ore, unpriced, unbought, is poured from
>   Veins unexhausted.
>
> They made confession of their open errors;
> Honestly told God of their secret follies;
> Afresh their service as true vassals pledged Him,
>   And then were merry.
>
> Strong was their purpose; nature made them nobles;
> Religion made them kings, to reign forever!
> Hymns of thanksgiving were their happy faces,
>   Beaming in music."

We shall find the same intense religious spirit manifest if we follow William Penn and his Quakers into New Jersey and Pennsylvania. Of all the founders of American life, none did more honor to Christianity than William Penn. Penn sought in the New World a refuge for his persecuted brethren. Having purchased his land of Charles II., in deference to the public law of the time, he proceeded, in obedience to the unwritten law in his own conscience, to re-purchase it from the Indians. If Penn's example had been followed throughout, in the treatment of the Indians, we would not have the dark, disgraceful history behind us which shames every student of the Indian question; neither would it be necessary for us to be, at present, massing troops in the Northwest, in anticipation of a new Indian war. The Indian kings gathered in council with the Quakers under the shades of the Burlington forests, and said, "You are our brothers, and we will live like brothers with you. We will have a broad path for you and us to walk in. If an Englishman falls asleep in this path, the Indian shall pass him by, and say, 'He is an Englishman; he is asleep; let him alone.' The path shall be plain; there shall not be in it a stump to hurt the feet."

Soon after the colony was founded, the genuineness of Penn's religion was tested in a very practical way. A company of traders offered six thousand pounds and an annual revenue for a monopoly of the Indian traffic between the Delaware and the Susquehanna. Penn at this time was in very straitened circumstances, and the temptation was great; but he held himself bound by his religion to equal laws, and rebuked the cupidity of monopoly. "I will not abuse the love of God," — such was his decision, — "nor act unworthy of his providence, by defiling what came to me clean. No; let the Lord guide me by his wisdom, to honor his name and serve his truth and people, that an example and a standard may be set up to the nations."

Penn's neighbor, Lord Baltimore, the founder of Maryland, was also moved to his adventures in the New World by a fervent desire to open a refuge for Roman Catholics, who in that day were as much persecuted in England as were the Quakers.

Oglethorpe, the founder of Georgia, was also a man of noble and splendid philanthropy, who sought to open a new field for the poor and unfortunate. Dr. Gray, whom I have already quoted, compares him to General Booth of the Salvation Army, and his great social scheme of founding colonies in South Africa of the rescued victims from the London slums. "No colony has so noble, so utterly unselfish, an origin, as the fair domain of Georgia, disgraced afterwards though it was by the conduct of men who had forced themselves into power. But this alone of all the thirteen was founded as a distinct attempt at wide and practical charity. This alone incorporated in its first charter a clause forbidding forever the traffic in slaves or spirituous liquors within its territorial bounds."

Not only did this spirit of intense reverence for religion have to do with the early explorations and founding of colonies in America, but it was a recognized factor in the beginning of our national councils.

In the Constitutional Convention in 1787, Benjamin Franklin, the prestige of whose great fame has been sometimes claimed by reckless champions of infidelity, moved " that henceforth prayers, imploring the assistance of Heaven and its blessings on our deliberations, be held in this Assembly every morning before we proceed to business." In the course of his short speech in support of this motion, he said: —

"In this situation of this Assembly, groping, as it were, in the dark to find political truth, and scarce able to distinguish it when presented to us, how has it happened, sir, that we have not hitherto once thought of humbly applying to the Father of Lights to illuminate our understandings? In the beginning of the contest with Britain, when we were sensible of danger, we had daily prayers in this room for the Divine protection. Our prayers, sir, were heard; and they were graciously answered. To that kind Providence we owe this happy opportunity of consulting in peace on the means of establishing our future national felicity. And have we now forgotten that powerful Friend? I have lived, sir, a long time; and the longer I live, the more convincing proofs I see of this truth, *that God governs in the affairs of men!* And if a sparrow cannot fall to the ground without his notice, is it probable that an empire can rise without his aid? We have been assured, sir, in the Sacred Writings, that 'except the Lord build the house, they labor in vain that build it.' I firmly believe this; and I also believe that, without his concurring aid, we shall succeed in this political building no better than in the building of Babel; we shall be divided by our little partial local interests, our projects will be confounded, and we ourselves shall become a reproach and a by-word down to future ages. And, what is worse, mankind may hereafter, from this unfortunate instance, despair of establishing government by human wisdom, and leave it to chance, war, and conquest."

It is a long march down hill from this sublime utterance of Franklin to the "phosphorescent and morally putrescent sentences" of Senator Ingalls, with which I began. America belongs to Christianity. Its discovery, colonization, and national development have all been pervaded by a spirit of reverence for Jesus Christ. The men who propose to open the Columbian World's Fair on the Sabbath, propose to do violence to the spirit of American history. The men who are trying to banish the Bible from the public schools are, at the least, indifferent to all the primal sources of our American national life. As Christian people we need to be loyal to the Christian history of our country. We are citizens of a continent which, from the White Mountains to the Sierra Nevadas, has been baptized in the name of Jesus. It is not only by the Hoang-ho, the Nile, or the Congo, that the missionary of the cross is the explorer of continents: it was as true of the Merrimac, the Susquehanna, the Ohio, the Mississippi, and the Columbia.

> "God bless our native land!
> Firm may she ever stand,
>   Through storm and night;
> When the wild tempests rave,
> Ruler of wind and wave,
> Do Thou our country save
>   By Thy great might!

For her our prayers shall rise
To God above the skies;
   On Him we wait;
Thou who art ever nigh,
Guarding with watchful eye
To Thee aloud we cry,
   God save the State!"

X

OUR BROTHER IN RED

"We are verily guilty concerning our brother." — *Gen.* xliii. 21.

FOR some weeks the daily newspapers have had startling head-lines about a threatened Indian war in the North-west. That there could be a possibility for such a war, is a sad reflection on American civilization. These Indians have all been born in America. They have been reared in the heart of our Government. On every side of them there has surged the life of our people. That we have failed to win their confidence and bind them to us by mutual ties of respect and good-will, is one of the saddest failures of our time.

The present excitement in the North-west has revived all the cruel and unjust proverbs about the Indian. "There is no good Indian but a dead Indian," has had the changes rung on it again *ad nauseam*. A few years since, it was my privilege, at a banquet in Tremont Temple, to hear that justly eminent man, Frederick

Douglass, respond to the toast, "A man's a man for a' that," when he was cheered to the echo.

We have learned to accept the truthfulness of Burns's proverb, when applied to the negro, and to call him "our brother in black;" but its practical disregard, when applied to the Indian, forms one of the darkest threads in the woof of our history. The common practice, even among well-meaning people, when the claims of the Indians are urged, of referring to some bloody atrocity committed by this or that tribe or body of Indians, as an answer to everything that may be said in their behalf, is not only pernicious, but cruelly unjust.

We have within the last five years, on several occasions, witnessed atrocities, equal to anything in Indian history, committed in the midst of the civilization of our great cities. We have seen the dynamite mangling of innocent victims; passenger trains, filled with women and children, thrown from the track; and brutal attacks made on honest, unoffending laborers. We do not brand the whole Irish or German races as anarchists and fiends because of this; we only say that this capacity for fiendishness is in every human race. No other race has had this capacity, in our day, so cruelly and so fully provoked as the Indian. When Columbus returned to Spain from his first voyage to America, he wrote a letter to Ferdinand and Isabella describing the new-found Americans, whom he named Indians, in which he says: "I swear to your majesties that there is not a better people in the world than these, — more affectionate, affable, or mild. They love their neighbors as themselves; their language is the sweetest, the softest, and the most cheerful, for they always speak smiling; and although they go naked, let your majesties believe me, their customs are very becoming. And their king, who is served with great majesty, has such engaging manners that it gives great pleasure to see him; and also to consider the great retentive faculty of that people, and their desire of knowledge, which incites them to ask the causes and effects of things."

There seems to be no reason for doubting that the term, now used in mockery, "the noble red man," was once appropriately applied. The Indian was a promising race, however he has been degraded by injustice, whiskey, and forced pauperism. And it may be doubted if the atrocities which at times have been committed by bands of Indians, maddened by "a century of dishonor," may not be paralleled by white atrocities, with Indian victims.

The spirit which the Western Indian very frequently meets with to-day may be inferred from the following extract from "Arizona and Sonora," by Sylvester Mowry. "There is only one way," says this proud representative of the higher civilization, "to wage war on the Apaches. A steady, persistent campaign must be made, following them to their haunts, hunting them to the fastnesses of the mountains. They must be surrounded, starved into coming in, surprised, or inveigled by white flags, or any other method, human or divine, and then put to death. If these ideas shock any weak-minded philanthropist, I can only say that I pity him without respecting his mistaken sympathy. A man might as well have sympathy for a rattlesnake or a tiger."

Is it to be wondered at that the Indian, robbed at every turn for generations; driven from place to place in herds at the beck of the on-pushing settler, who, in his treatment of the Indian, is frequently a "border ruffian" indeed; pursued relentlessly by a spirit of which the quotation I have just given is an example, — is it to be wondered at that the milder graces of Christian character are of tardy growth under such treatment?

Take the case of the Sioux, about whom gathers the present excitement. When Captain Carver was travelling among the North American Indians, during the years 1766 and 1767, he was most hospitably entertained for seven months by the forefathers of the present Sioux. And he assures us that when the time came for him to depart, three hundred of them accompanied him for a distance on his journey, and took leave with expressions of friendship for him and good-will toward the great father, the English king, of whom he had told them. The chiefs wished him to say to the king, "How much we desire that traders may be sent to abide among us, with such things as we need, that the hearts of our young men, our wives and children may be made glad. And may peace subsist between us so long as the sun, the moon, the earth, and the waters shall endure." Seventy years later, when the artist Catlin made his journeys among the North-American Indians, he spent several weeks among the Sioux, and says of them: "There is no tribe on the continent of finer-looking men, and few tribes who are better and more comfortably clad and supplied with the necessaries of life. I have travelled several years already among these people, and I have not had my scalp taken, nor a blow struck me, nor had occasion to raise my hand against an Indian; nor has my property been stolen as yet to my knowledge to the value of a shilling, and that in a country where no man is punishable by law for the crime of stealing. That the Indians in their native state are drunken, is false, for they are the only temperance people, literally speaking, that ever I saw in my travels, or expect to see. If the civilized world are startled at this, it is the fact that they must battle with, not with me. These people manufacture no spirituous liquors themselves, and know nothing of it until it is brought into their country and tendered to them by Christians."

I have been assured by army officers, conversant with Indian affairs, that no Indians in the country have been lied to, and tricked, so much as the Sioux. Helen Hunt Jackson, that most heroic friend of the Indian, tells how the Government was once forced, against the will of the Indian Commissioner, to keep its contract with the famous Sioux chief, Spotted Tail. The Red Cloud and Spotted Tail bands consented to go to the old Ponca Reserve, only after being told that all their supplies had been sent to a certain point on the Missouri River with a view to this move; and, it being too late to take all this freight northward again, they would starve if they stayed where they were. They were given a written pledge from the Government that they would be allowed to go back in the spring. In the spring, no orders came for the removal. March passed, April passed — no orders. Finally, in May, the Commissioner of Indian Affairs went himself to hold a council with them. When he rose to speak, the chief, Spotted Tail, sprang up, walked toward him, waving in his hand the paper containing the promise of the Government to return them to White Clay Creek, and exclaimed, "All the men who come from Washington are liars, and the bald-headed ones are the worst of all! I don't want to hear one word from you; you are a bald-headed old liar. You have but one thing to do here, and that is to give an order for us to return to White Clay Creek. Here are your written words; and if you don't give this order, and everything here is not on wheels inside of ten days, I'll order my young men to tear down and burn everything in this part of the country! I don't want to hear anything more from you, and I've got nothing more to say to you." And he turned his back on the Commissioner and walked away. Such language as this would not have been borne from unarmed and helpless Indians, but when it came from a chief with four thousand armed warriors at his back, it was another affair altogether. The order was written. In less than ten days everything was "on wheels," and the whole body of these Sioux on the move to the country they had indicated. The Secretary of the Interior said, very naïvely, in his report for that year: "The Indians were found to be quite determined to move westward, and the promise of the Government in that respect was faithfully kept." Little praise the Government deserved for keeping its promises under the circumstances!

In dealing with the Indians the policy of the Government has been to treat them like children in forcing them into contracts and treaties, and then hold them to the strictest responsibility for violation. The *New York Examiner*, in an editorial article last week, furnishes an example of the unfair attitude of public sentiment toward the Indian. This editor, speaking of the present situation, says: " The power behind the whole movement is Sitting Bull. He is a great chief, blessed with a 'heap' of cunning. He has a fondness for engineering any enterprise against the whites. In addition to the natural antipathy, he has a grudge against our Government for pressing the cession of eleven millions of acres of the Sioux reservation. Sitting Bull signed the agreement of transfer only when undue pressure was brought to bear. He appended his signature under protest, and with muttered threats of revenge." Of course it is certain proof of the fiendishness of Sitting Bull's character and the general unregenerate condition of his heart, that he isn't ready to fall down and worship the people who took him by the throat and forced him to sign away his right to eleven million acres of land, the title of which had been vested in his tribe and guaranteed to it by the honor of the United States Government!

Let the same scheme be tried on some Baptist deacon in New England, and see how much of love and affection there will be welling up in his soul for the people who hold a pistol at his head and force him under "undue pressure" to deed away his homestead "under protest."

On last Wednesday, when the joint resolution came up in the United States Senate, authorizing the Secretary of War to furnish arms and ammunition to the North-western States, Mr. Voorhees for the Democrats and Mr. Hawley for the Republicans united in the declaration that if the proposition were one to issue a hundred thousand rations of food to the starving Indians, it would be more consistent with Christian civilization. Major-General Miles has recently stated in public interviews that the Indians are being driven to revolt by starvation, and that they prefer to die fighting, rather than to starve peacefully.

General Miles gives it as his judgment that it is an inexpiable crime on the part of the Government to stand silently by and do nothing except furnish arms to the whites.

From what I have seen personally of the unscrupulous greed of many frontier settlers to get possession of the Indian lands, I fully agree with Senator Voorhees, who, in his reply to Senator Pierce of Dakota, declared that he would take the statement of General Miles far sooner than that of a senator who lived near the Sioux reservation, and who, with his people, wanted to get the Indian lands as soon as possible. "The one was a reliable officer; the other was the fox lying around the pen where the geese were, waiting to get some of them."

All the Indian troubles of recent times have been brought about by injustice on the part of the whites. Our last great Indian war was that against the Nez Perces, under their famous chief, Joseph. Joseph and myself were born and reared in sight of the same great mountains. He is only a few years older than I. Those mountains are as dear to me as to him, and I could not restrain the tears when I read his plea to the army officers when he was confined down in the flat, sickly Indian Territory. "Give me just one little mountain," said Joseph, "and I will die content." Joseph fought for that which the white man calls patriotism when it has been crowned with success. Joseph's fathers received all the early explorers and settlers with a broad generosity and manly fellowship. They prided themselves on having received Lewis and Clarke, Bonneville, Fremont, and other white men, with the hand of friendship, and on never having falsified their promises. Up to the time of Joseph's outbreak, though a number of Nez Perces had been killed by white men, only one white man had ever fallen at the hand of a Nez Perce. Joseph's father joined with the other independent chiefs in a formal treaty concluded in the Walla Walla Valley, in 1855, by which the Indians gave up all claims to certain large tracts of lands.

Old Joseph entered into this contract only on the express stipulation that the Wallowa and Imnaha valleys should remain to him and his children forever. Soon the white men wanted these valleys, and another treaty was made with several chiefs, but Joseph refused to have anything to do with it, and was not even present; but these valleys, that had been guaranteed to Joseph on the honor of the United States Government, were by this new treaty taken from him. Joseph's own parable, by which he illustrated the brutal injustice of this treatment, cannot be improved upon. Said he: "A man comes to me and says, 'Joseph, I like your horses, and I want to buy them.' I say I do not want to sell them. He goes to my neighbor and says, 'Joseph has some good horses, but he will not sell them;' and my neighbor says, 'Pay me, and you may have them.' And he does so, and then comes to me and says, 'Joseph, I have bought your horses.'" But despite all justice and reason, marauders poured into these beautiful valleys, the home of his youth, and United States troops were sent to compel Joseph and his people to remove to a strange reservation. Imagine the agony of brave-hearted men and women in an emergency like that. And yet, with breaking heart, Joseph concluded to move. In his own language he says: "I said in my heart that rather than have war, I would give up my country, I would give up my father's grave; I would give up everything, rather than have the blood of white men on the hands of my people." It was not easy for Joseph to bring his people to consent to move. The young men wished to fight. At this time Chief Joseph rode one day through his village with a revolver in each hand, saying he would shoot the first one of his warriors to resist the Government. Finally they gathered together their herds of cattle and horses, and began to move. A storm came and raised the river so high that some of the cattle could not be taken across.

Indian guards were put in charge of the cattle left behind. White men attacked these guards and drove away the cattle. Joseph could no longer restrain his men. That was the birth of the Nez Perce Indian war. Put yourself in the place of Joseph, and blame him if you can. Nothing in the history of modern warfare surpasses in daring, genius, and bravery, the exploits of Joseph, the Nez Perce chief.

"Defeated in a bitterly contested battle, he led his great caravan of two thousand horses or more, on which were women, children, old men, and old women, the wounded, palsied, and blind, by a seemingly impassable trail, interlaced with fallen trees, through the ruggedest mountains, to the Bitter Root Valley, where he made a treaty of forbearance with the inhabitants, passing by settlements containing banks and stores, and near farms rich with stock, but taking nothing and hurting no one. So he pushed on; he crossed the Rocky Mountains twice, the Yellowstone and the Missouri rivers, and was within one day's march of Canada when he was taken." During all this time the United States Government had thousands of soldiers in the field, under skilful and experienced officers like Generals Howard and Miles, and had spent millions of dollars in coping with this brave young hero. Yes, why not say hero? If we were speaking of Roman or Grecian wars, or of the exploits of some Garibaldi or Kossuth, we should consider it something magnificent in a race crushed, broken, overwhelmed by a hundred years of conquest, that it should still be able to inspire fear and compel respect for its patriotic devotion to the home of its ancestry. If Joseph had been of less noble spirit, he need never have suffered capture. He himself says: " We could have escaped if we had left our wounded behind. We were unwilling to do this. We had never heard of a wounded Indian recovering while in the hands of white men."

A little company did slip away, and escaped across the line; and when the Government sent a commission over there to ask them to come back, a squaw named "The-One-That-Speaks-Once," and wife of "The-Man-That-Scatters-The-Bear," stood up in the council and said: "I was over at your country. I wanted to raise my children over there, but you did not give me any time. I came over to this country to raise my children, and have a little peace." It ought to make every American's cheek to blush, when he contrasts the history of the Indians of Canada with that of those in the United States. There are one hundred thousand Indians in Canada, yet, with the exception of the little flurry with the half-breeds, a few years since, the Canadians have had no Indian trouble.

Over there they are called " the Indian subjects of her Majesty," are held amenable to the law, and are protected by the law. Bishop Whipple, than whom we have no wiser student of the Indian question, says: " On one side of the line is a nation that has spent five hundred million dollars in Indian wars, a people who have not a hundred miles between the Atlantic and Pacific which has not been the scene of a massacre; a government which has not passed twenty years without an Indian war; not one Indian tribe to whom it has given a Christian civilization; and which celebrated its centenary by another Indian war. On the other side of the line are the same greedy, dominant, Anglo-Saxon race, and the same heathen; yet they have not spent one dollar in Indian wars, and they never have had a massacre."

There is nothing so costly as injustice. No man, no nation, can ever escape the penalty for unjust treatment of the ignorant and the helpless. The victim of oppression has for an avenger One whose arms are stronger than the might of armies. In the words of Helen Hunt Jackson, in her song of " Mordecai," I would say of the Indian what she says of the despised Jew, —

"Make friends with him ! He is of royal line,
Although he sits in rags.
Make friends with him, for unawares
The charmed secret of thy joys he bears ;
Be glad, so long as his black sackcloth, late
And early, thwarts thy sun ; for if in hate
And haste thou plottest for his blood, thy own death-cry,
Not his, comes from the gallows fifty cubits high."

SERMON FRAGMENTS

I

THE WRECKAGE AND SALVAGE OF MODERN CITIES

"The voice of the Lord calleth unto the city." — *Mic.* vi. 9.

THE interest of history clusters about great cities. The history of the ancient world is the history of Nineveh and Babylon and Jerusalem, of Rome and Athens and Alexandria. The modern European world has its destinies dictated by London, Paris, Berlin, and St. Petersburg. Our own country is no exception; the history of the American people gathers about the Puritans of Boston, the Knickerbockers of New York, the Creoles of New Orleans, the Quakers of Philadelphia, and the Argonauts of San Francisco. There is something in the hurrying life of the city that fascinates and holds the multitudes of men and women. There is in the modern city not only much of salvage, but many saving characteristics. The strongest and noblest intellectual fibre in men and women is developed in cities. Emerson said: "A scholar is a candle which the love and desire of all men will light." The human mind needs the stimulus of fellowship with many kindred minds to make luxuriant growths. The brain receives its brightest polish where gold and silver lose theirs. The broadest and tenderest charity is developed in cities. Mr. Howells, in his novel, "The Minister's Charge," makes Lemuel Barker say: "If any one happens to find out that you are in trouble, there's ten times as much done for you in the city as in the country;" and when Evans, the shrewd Boston editor, replied, "Perhaps that is because there are ten times as many to do it;" Lemuel replied, "No, it isn't that altogether. It's because they have seen ten times as much trouble, and know how to take hold of it better." Sympathy is not only developed, but made wise and skilful, by contact with the wants and sorrows of humanity.

The most active, self-denying piety is developed in the cities. The same general law that produces the brightest merchants, the most skilful mechanics, in the city, develops also the most active and diligent Christian. They ship splendid pieces of timber from the Puget Sound forests to all the ship-building ports of the globe, to be used as masts on the great ocean-carrying vessels. Where do they get those long straight pieces, one hundred and fifty feet without a knot, or a twist, or a flaw of any kind, straight as an arrow, and faultless as a chiselled statue? Surely not on some skirmish line of straggling trees, standing lonesomely to face the storms of winter. No, indeed; they go back into the depths of the woods, where thousands of trees grow as regularly side by side as ever a regiment of trained soldiers stood shoulder to shoulder on dress parade. So the heart and soul of every great reformation has had its birth in the great cities.

But the city has its wreckers and its wreckage as well. First and foremost as the chief wrecker in our modern cities, any honest observer is compelled to put the saloon. It is not only the drunkenness it causes, not only the army of criminals and paupers and idiots that follows in its wake; but the city dram-shop has a moral poison for the whole community about it. Every profane and vulgar and irreverent impulse is fed and fattened in its stenchful atmosphere. It is the headquarters of all the festering elements of political corruption and municipal misrule. It is the recruiting station of pauperism. I have followed men in five different cities, to whom I gave small sums of money to get something to eat, in answer to their plea of hunger, and in every instance I traced them directly to the saloon and saw them squander it in strong drink. Then there is the wreckage of lust. The White Cross societies have come none too soon. God speed the White Cross and its heroic band of workers, and give them a lasting influence on the minds of the youth of the country! But in the meantime there is need for an awakened public conscience, that will demand that the abominable traffic in the virtue of young girls be stopped. The injustice and oppression in wages which young women suffer has much to do with the wreckage of lust. An examination of two thousand cases of women who had fallen into a bad life, revealed the fact that only five per cent had received as much as $8 per week. Twenty-seven only received $6 per week. One hundred and twenty-six received $4 per week; 230, $3 per week; 336, $2 per week; and 534 had fought the losing battle on $1 per week. In the investigation made by the Central Labor Bureau of Boston, relating to the employment of children and girls, some startling facts were developed, showing how young girls are pushed with a strong hand toward lives of infamy. Instances were cited of firms that paid $50,000 a year for advertising, and only $2 per week for girls who came to them from the high school.

Then there is in our American cities the drift wreckage from foreign shores. Here in our own Boston, not a single house only, or a single block, but whole streets and sections of the city, — once, from end to end, the abode of the most industrious, the most intelligent, and wholesome of American citizenship, — have been ingulfed and swallowed up in the drift wreckage from the worst elements of Old-World cities. As yet we have done next to nothing in attacking with our Protestant gospel these Old-World settlements in our modern cities. Often we stand before them ready to say: "Can these dry bones live?" But the voice of God comes to us, saying: "Though ye have lain among the pots, yet ye shall be as the wings of a dove covered with silver, and her feathers with yellow gold."

This wreckage shall become salvage when the American churches, with faith and self-denial, give themselves up to the work of seeking out and saving the lost. A dignified, aristocratic church will never save this world. But a sympathetic, loving, self-denying church, that is willing to go into the depths as Christ did, can save it.

II

CHRIST'S SYMPATHY FOR CITIES

"And when he was come near, he beheld the city, and wept over it." — *Luke* xix. 41.

JESUS introduced into the world a new estimate of the value of humanity, and necessarily assumed with it a new attitude toward humanity itself. The man who, for a pretence, made long prayers, the selfish lawyers, who bound heavy burdens on the populace, had only contempt for the masses of the city. Jesus, who came to help, to lift burdens from weary shoulders, was full of respect and sympathy for the humblest soul. These two standards — that of the selfish worldling, or his near kinsman, the aristocratic Pharisee, and that of Jesus — stand ever against each other in eternal antagonism. Illustrations are not lacking. The afternoon of the last session of the Board of Trade of Chicago for September, 1888, revealed a unique and suggestive contrast. It was the afternoon when the wheat broker known as "Old Hutch" clasped his withered hands tightly around the necks of hundreds of ruined men, and sent them despairing and desperate to their sorrowing homes, — all this that he might add another superfluous million to the millions whose very income he is unable to use. A brighter picture, however, was presented at the door of the Board of Trade that afternoon. A negro boy, who makes his living blacking boots for the brokers, brought the result of his week's work, in dimes and nickels and coppers, and with beaming face laid the little heap down upon the table of the chief officer of the city as his contribution to the yellow-fever sufferers of Jacksonville, Florida. There in the black-faced boot-black you have the Christ attitude toward humanity, while in the other instance you have the incarnation of worldly selfishness. When the centenary of Stephenson, the engineer, was celebrated not long since at Newcastle-on-Tyne, there was a great procession; but a little company of workingmen from the village where Stephenson was born attracted most attention by a simple banner on which was inscribed the motto: "He was one of us." The day will come when the workingmen of the world will carry the white flag of the Cross, and be proudest of all to say of Jesus, their noblest friend, "He was one of us."

The attitude of the modern church toward the

city of to-day ought to be the same as that of Jesus to the city of old. Christ wept over the sorrows and wants of the city. He did not contemplate the struggling masses of men and women with long homilies on the survival of the fittest, or exhortations on social statistics. Jesus had a heart. When he looked down on the seething masses of suffering, sinning men and women, he wept over them. He could not restrain himself. He broke down in sobs and tears. Some people imagine it a sign of weakness to be so moved by the world's trouble as to cry over it. May we have more of the heavenly weakness! It is the weakness of great souls. Narrow, indifferent, selfish souls can survey the agony of wrecked and desolate lives, and go calmly on their way. But hearts made tender by the spirit of Jesus will often contemplate the city with broken hearts and wet eyes.

The modern church needs to get near to people, as Jesus did. The churches of this city have a great responsibility on their hands in caring for the tens of thousands of young men and women who come to Boston from the towns and villages and farms of all these New England States.

We must hunt out these boys and girls who have wandered from Christian homes, and are being overcome and destroyed by the wickedness of the city, — who are feeding their homesick souls on the gilded but poisoned vices of the world; we must hold out to them the old Bible and the old faith with winning sympathy, and say: "Here is the bread of life that fed your mother, a loaf from the dear old oven of your childhood."

III

IN DARKEST ENGLAND AND THE WAY OUT, WITH BOSTON APPLICATIONS

"A land of darkness, as darkness itself, and of the shadow of death, without any order, and where the light is darkness." — *Job* x. 22.

THE text of General Booth's sermon given to us in this helpful book, is the great Congo forest in the heart of Africa, where Stanley left so many of his disheartened followers. In the unique sermon of the Salvationist general, the dark forest stands for the slum region of the great cities. The indomitable Stanley represents the moral leaders, the Christian workers, who dare to go down in the darkness to rescue the lost. Emin, doubtful, vacillating, not knowing whether he wants to be rescued or not, stands for the poor victims of this dark wilderness. General Booth not only plans and pleads for help for the semi-respectable, who are largely able to take care of themselves, but bravely says, "No one will make even a visible dint on the morass of squalor, who does not deal with the improvident, the lazy, the vicious, and the criminal." The terrible fact needs to be emphasized, that we in Boston, in several sections of the city, are deliberately breeding a vicious class that bids fair to be equal in degradation to anything London can show to-day. During the past week, within five minutes' walk of the pulpit where I now stand, I have visited more than one "chamber of horrors." Block after block, on certain streets, is given up to vileness of every description. Many of these old rookeries are not fit for any one to live in. They are nest-holes of vermin and disease. Children are growing up in these places, who have not been born into the world so much as "damned into the world." I went into miserable holes, miscalled homes, where on the coldest day of last week the windows were broken, no fire, no coal, nothing to eat, little children shivering in rags, and the mother drunk. In these places the beds are often only a pile of worn straw and rags on the floor, covered with a ragged, filthy, vermin-inhabited comforter. One wonders if it is possible that the Board of Health ever visits these places. Since an improper play was driven from the stage of a Boston theatre, because of the personal investigation of the officers granting the license, I have had some hope that if the city officials could be stirred up to personally investigating these foul regions, something might be done toward cleansing them. Yet, in the midst of this horrible section, there is a cluster of four saloons that manage to filch enough out of these people to pay annually six thousand dollars in license money. In one large family, crowded into three little rooms, where there are three of the family who work, the mother admitted to the officer that they spent twelve dollars a week for ale and beer, which is nearly ten times as much as they pay for rent. The children growing up in these places do not go to school. There are young men and women who have grown up there who are unable to read or write. They are accustomed, from their infancy, to every form of vice and crime. They talk about "going down to the Island," as nonchalantly as decent people do about going to the post-office.

These slums are a disgrace to Boston. They are not necessary. They ought to be cleansed out of existence. The children in every one of these families, accustomed to figure in the police court, ought to be taken at once out of these haunts of darkness. Shall we not have, with all our organizations, a new one, or, rather, a sort of federation of all the others, that shall have for its one object the utter annihilation of the slums?

IV

THE MISSION OF THE INKHORN

"Behold, six men came, . . . and every man a slaughter weapon; and one man among them was clothed with linen, with a writer's inkhorn by his side." — *Ezek.* ix. 2.

THERE were six men on this mission of judgment to a great city. Each man carried a slaughter weapon. What particular kind of weapons the other five had, we do not know; but this reporter who was clothed in linen, and carried an inkhorn at his side, we cannot doubt that his weapon was his pen. That the pen is a slaughter weapon, all history is full of proof. Louis Philippe of France was stabbed to death by the pens of his time. And that other Louis, whom Victor Hugo made the laughing-stock of the world as Napoleon the Little, shared a similar fate. Although Hugo was an exile without a refuge, a tramp without a passport, he was more than a match for the emperor on his throne. By the aid of his pen alone, he avenged the imprisoned and assassinated cause of human liberty. He dragged the usurper, emperor though he was, to the bar of public judgment, and there scourged him into contemptible insignificance for his crime against the chartered rights of the French people. The pens of William Lloyd Garrison and Harriet Beecher Stowe did more than battalions of bayonets to cut the throat of the slave power in America. They, indeed, made the battalions possible. It was the keen pen of a New York journalist that pierced the Tweed ring of New York City to the heart, and let in the light of day upon that writhing nest of political thieves. Alas! that all the slaughter of the pen is not of this kind. What an unrivalled blessing the pen and the press would be to mankind if their keen-edged blade was raised in menace only against tyranny and wrong, and ever in defence of liberty and truth!

The pen has never been so great a power in the history of the race as now. The streams that flow from it in newspapers, magazines, and books, are soon to water the entire heart of man with their influence, good or bad. No cause can afford to be indifferent in regard to the position of the public prints. First and foremost to-day the influence of the pen is felt in the daily newspapers. Dr. Munger has said: "If we were to send to the next planetary neighbor our most representative thing, I think it would be a book." But, for our age, it seems to me that the daily newspaper is still more representative. It represents the push, the nervous, restless, inventive activity of our time. Some one has said that men resort more and more to the sea, in search of all that is costly and desirable. In like manner do we depend more and more upon the newspaper for inexhaustible riches. The salt sea and the newspaper sea have both been so thoroughly utilized that they now diffuse their benign influence over the whole earth. And yet, we are all conscious that in many respects the influence of much of the daily press is not benign. I know that it is easy to retort that editors know more about newspaper making than clergymen, but the editors often give us advice about sermon making and the conduct of our church life. I do not see why we may not be mutually helpful.

A great newspaper is an affair of too much moment to be regarded as simply a scheme for private money-making. It is like a great river, which no man or corporation may buy or own; it is a highway for all the people, and on its bosom floats the commerce of a nation. So a great newspaper must be regarded as something broader than the man who owns it, or the individuals who edit it. The people who have the purity of society on their hearts have a right to expect that the momentous power of the daily press shall be exercised with reference to its influence on the morals of the community. We have a right to demand that our daily banquet for the intellectual entertainment and development of old and young in our homes, shall be something better than great barbecues of crime, even though they be served with every attraction of art. All honor to those noble men, who, resisting all the tremendous temptations to competition in this class of journalism, keep their pages pure and wholesome, put vice in the background, and the great interests of human life and government to the front.

One of the most dangerous features of modern city literature is the sensational novel of the lower class, which is so carefully worded as to be protected by law, yet carries blood-poison in every line. I am credibly informed that we have in our midst large publishing houses who hire the shrewdest legal ability, to whom is submitted the copy of these vile stories; and they are made just as unclean as possible and yet escape the pillory of the law. These publications flood the news-stands, and are pushed under the doors of our homes. I have seen men loaded down with mule-loads of this vile stuff, illustrated with vicious pictures, standing at the doors of the public-school buildings, distributing it to the boys and girls as they swarm out on their way home. Will our law-makers never learn wisdom? This blood-poisoning of children cannot go on without producing terrible results. Herod's murder of the innocents has its parallel in our own great cities at this very hour. While it is our duty to use every possible effort to have our present laws amended for the protection of the young, I would impress it upon parents that the great relief and antidote is good literature in the home. The man who has plenty of beefsteak and potatoes in his own dining-room is not likely to go nosing among the garbage tubs of his neighbors. Let the home abound in bright, fresh literature, that shall give a high tone and taste to the minds of our youth.

V

THE VICTORY AND PROMISE OF AMERICAN PATRIOTISM

(Decoration Day, 1890.)

"If I forget thee, O Jerusalem, let my right hand forget her cunning. If I do not remember thee, let my tongue cleave to the roof of my mouth, if I prefer not Jerusalem above my chief joy." — *Ps.* cxxxvii. 5, 6.

WE come this morning to pay our annual tribute of praise and gratitude to the hundreds of thousands of men who, in the hour of the nation's peril, gave their lives for its unity and its life. The monarchists of the Old World sneered that America was a nation of traders; that with the exception of the chivalry of the Southern plantations, her men had no soul above a cashier's desk or a dry-goods counter. Then suddenly the sneer is interrupted with the angry boom of a cannon aimed at the national flag; and lo! these traders and traffickers marched an army under the assaulted flag, such as the world had never beheld before. A navy springs into existence, such as up to that time the oceans had never carried.

But we would do less than our duty to-day if we did not remember that days of peace have their demands for a patriotism as unselfish and heroic as times of war. We are facing problems to-day that will test to the last extremity the sincerity of our loyalty to our country and its institutions. Here is what we call the "Southern problem." When the end of the war came, the country admitted the negro into the brotherhood of American citizenship, and pledged him an equal chance under the law; that pledge has never been made good. But we have Northern problems as well. When it is possible for a coal trust to cause settlers on the Western prairies to freeze to death for fuel, or a flour trust to impoverish the Eastern poor, we may be sure there is room for the keen eyes of patriotism to search into the problems of our financial and social life. The problem of city misrule, mixed up as it is with the unrestricted dumping of European sewage into our great cities, which speedily develops into political power, lays a great weight of obligation upon our patriotism. The presence of this Ladies' Relief Corps to-day suggests the tremendous debt the Government owes to the loyal women of the nation, who, in home and manufactory and hospital, made victory possible. These American women deserve the ballot, and the Government cannot afford to go without this splendid reserve force of moral power.

I have faith in the future of our country. I believe the patriotism of the twentieth century will be the grandest type the world has seen.

VI

THE EXTRAVAGANCE AND BRUTALITY OF MODERN SPORTS

"A merry heart doeth good like a medicine."— *Prov.* xvi. 22.

"Do thyself no harm." — *Acts* xvi. 28.

PAUL, who was the author of the second scripture, was, at the time of its utterance, a very happy illustration of the first proverb, showing the value of a cheerful heart in the most trying experiences.

The man who could have "a good time" in spite of the midnight dungeon and binding fetters, carried something about with him that was worth having. The Bible does not set itself against amusement, or innocent, helpful sport. Men and women need and must have some kind of recreation. We carry in ourselves, by the very charter of our creation, the right to pleasure from many sources. We are as certainly equipped for enjoyment as for labor. The human body is constructed like some delicate musical instrument which may be pitched to a thousand joyous tunes. The eye, the ear, the mouth, indeed every organ and sense, are so many windows through which we may enjoy the beauties of the world. Christianity does not undertake to quench this desire for recreation, but to control and direct it into safe and healthful channels.

But from the Puritan extreme, which would suppress all amusements, we are threatened with anarchy in the world of recreation, which, instead of recreating, would destroy both body and soul. The tendency to brutality in the public popular sports of the last few years cannot but be a serious reflection to any thoughtful mind. The decline of Roman greatness, the precursor of her disintegration and ruin, was signalized by bloody and cruel games. Reverence for life is one of the surest indications of civilization. Sensitiveness to the feeling or sufferings of another is the highest type of human life. But we have whole circles of society to whom the prize-ring represents the highest ideal of human enjoyment. The newspapers have columns every day served up for their delectation. I hold in my hand clippings of the past week or so in different parts of the country giving accounts of men who beat each other into painful wounds, in some cases into insensibility, for the sport — the so-called recreation — of other men. One of the saddest of facts is that the enjoyment of this brutal amusement is not confined to the ignorant and vicious classes only, but these brutal human mills are attended by many men who are supposed to be creditable members of society. When the big brute Sullivan went over to England, the Prince of Wales did him the honor to call upon him and pay him the courtesy of a private audience. The most honored educator in America would not have been so favored by the heir of England's throne. What a window this is into the heart of society, showing how much of brutality, fierce and wolfish, is still shut under the hatches of moral and legal restraint! The *Pall Mall Gazette* says the police can put down prize-fighting, but the prize-fighting cult, the worship of the man with a sixteen-inch biceps as the ideal man, remains as strong as ever. It is against that spirit of brutality that all good men and women must set themselves. One of the most significant illustrations of this brutal tendency may be seen in the college and popular games of the time. I hold in my hands the clippings of two weeks that show, in the record of ball games alone, one boy fatally shot, one youth whose neck was broken, one nose broken, and scores of broken fingers, scalp wounds, and blackened eyes.

The recent outrage committed by some of the students of Harvard College is an illustration of this spirit; and the remark of one of the young men at the mass meeting of students hit the mark exactly, — "that if the public sentiment in the college had not been very low, such an outrage would have been impossible."

As this tendency to brutality in sports increases, extravagance increases as well. A successful base-ball pitcher commands a salary as large, or nearly so, as the Governor of the commonwealth, and through the summer season receives more attention from the public press. The national game is becoming in many respects a great gambling hell, where pools are sold as at a horse-race. Yachting has become one of the common sports in which large amounts of money are spent.

Now, I do not speak as the enemy of outdoor amusements. I speak only in warning against that extravagance which means harm, and in many cases overthrow. The great purpose of life, after all, is not merely to "have a good time," but to build up a noble character and to honestly serve one's age. The danger to young people especially is that they will get an extravagant idea of the importance of what is, after all, only incidental to the serious and important mission of humanity.

VII

THE CAUSES OF SUICIDE

"And when Ahithophel saw that his counsel was not followed, he saddled his ass and arose and got him home to his house, to his city, and put his household in order, and hanged himself." — 2 *Sam.* xvii. 23.

THE question of suicide is becoming a very important one, since nearly seven thousand persons have committed self-murder in this country alone during the past year. There has been a commonly accepted opinion in this country, that our American spirit of restlessness is responsible for this increase in the frequency of suicide, but the facts do not bear out this position. The most recent figures carefully ascertained by responsible scientists prove that self-destruction is increasing as rapidly in other civilized countries, whose citizens have never been accused of overwork, as in America. The cause lies deeper, in the estimate that is put upon human life. A materialistic, sensual age would naturally be specially open to this temptation. Who has not noticed the utter recklessness of life shown by many Anarchists and Nihilists? It is a desperation that springs not only from their sense of wrong, but its chief bitterness lies in their lack of faith in the immortality of man or the justice of God. The heathen Yang Choo comforts his disciples with this: "All are born, and all die. The virtuous and the sage die; the ruffian and the fool also die. Alive they were Yaon and Shun, the most virtuous of men; dead, they are so much rotten bone. Or, alive they were Clee and Chow, the most wicked of men; dead, they are so much rotten bone." Spread that belief generally among mankind, and you will multiply all crimes against the person, and suicide as rapidly as any.

Another cause of suicide in our time is the fierce competition for wealth and position; the false conviction that places specially conspicuous are places of great happiness; a thirst for display, leading men and women to live beyond their means, that they may seem to their fellows to have more wealth than they really possess. After the waste comes bankruptcy, sometimes in money only, often in both money and reputation, and the character having been already squandered, there remains the halter of Ahithophel, or the pistol of the defaulter. The slavery of vice and the remorseful sting of sin often cause suicide. The wine-cup and the gambling-hell help largely to swell the list of suicides. There is no remedy for the increase of suicide except the development of a pure faith and life among men and women. Prove to a man that life is a divine gift given for noble ends, and develop in him a love of pure things, and he would as soon take the life of an angel as the life of a man. Degrade a man in faith and life until he seems to himself only an animal that eats and drinks and dies, and he will slay a man with as little compunction as he would take the life of a sheep.

VIII

THE AGE OF THE LIAR

"Wherefore, putting away lying, speak every man truth with his neighbor, for we are members one of another." — *Eph.* iv. 25.

THE importance of truthfulness is indicated in the last sentence of the text. Truth is the bond that holds the world together. Men sail their ships, plant their crops, in fact, expend money and exertion in every possible department of life, because they have faith in the truthfulness of God.

Truth is the bond that holds society together. Business could not be carried on unless men had faith that contracts would be carried out. Any tendency in the age that indicates a decadence in truthfulness is therefore of serious importance.

The materialistic tendency of our time, the rapid building up of fortunes, the fast growth of population, and the sudden springing up of mighty cities, — all these tend to give men an exaggerated idea of the worth of material things, so that expediency often takes the place of truthfulness, and the miserable lying proverb, "The end justifies the means," becomes very popular in many circles.

We see this tendency to dissimulation, pretence, and exaggeration, in business circles. We have numerous large business houses in the city who for years have been advertising that they sell goods below cost. These firms make enormous fortunes by selling goods for less than they pay for them! Now, then, these men would be grossly insulted if you said, "You lie, gentlemen;" and yet there is, to say the least, a great carelessness about the truth of such statements.

The same tendency to the lack of sincerity may be seen in religious matters. In religion we call it "cant." In religion it should certainly be expected we should have perfect sincerity; and yet there, as well as in the counting-room and parlor, is a great temptation to follow the fashionable rut.

Young men and young women can do nothing better for themselves, even for this world alone, than to cultivate sincere, true characters.

It is only pure gold that stands testing by time; and truthfulness is not only the cement that binds society together, but it is the magnetism that holds the individual character in permanence.

IX

THE STRUGGLE BETWEEN THE AMERICAN AND FOREIGN SABBATH

"Can two walk together except they be agreed?" — *Amos* iii. 3.

THIS country is at present the theatre of a mighty struggle which is going on between two antagonistic ideas concerning the Sabbath. It is easy to find fault with our Puritan forefathers, and point out extravagances in the severity with which they enforced their ideas of Sabbath-keeping, but it is not so easy to parallel the race of noble men and women their system produced. The Puritan Sabbath, softened by a tenderer theology, gives what I call the American Sabbath — a day of mingled rest and worship. The flood of immigration from the Old World has brought with it the Continental Sabbath, a gala day — at the best, a single service in the morning, and a beer-garden in the afternoon; at the worst, a day of carousal for the rich, and unresting toil for the poor. The workingmen of this country are the last people who should favor Sabbath desecration; for the experience of history is that a Sunday of carousal and pleasure, in the course of a generation or two, becomes a Sunday of toil for working people. The American Sabbath, with its reverential spirit, its opportunities for rest and for religious teaching, cannot be lost out of our society without great harm and loss. The argument that Sunday excursions and pleasure jaunts are necessary for the health of the poor and overworked is largely sophistical. A wide experience among the poor people of cities leads me to say most positively that the healthiest people among them, man for man and family for family, are the earnest Christians who spend their Sundays in church-going. Such people on their Sabbaths get a breath of new thought and spiritual exaltation which is worth more physically to their tired nerves than even the breath of the sea or the fragrance of the forest.

X

NO MISSION TO GHOSTS

[Boston Herald Report.]

THOSE who attended the morning service at St. John's M. E. Church, Broadway, South Boston, yesterday, to listen to a sermon by the pastor, Rev. Louis Albert Banks, on "Hagar's Well of Water," were also treated to a discourse on a timely topic which was not down on the programme. As the pastor rose to deliver his sermon, he said that before taking up the theme of the morning he desired to read a letter which he had received through the mail, criticising his remarks in behalf of the striking carpenters the previous Sunday evening. The letter is as follows: —

MR. BANKS, — What consummate fools you preachers do make of yourselves in speaking of the labor question as you do. I speak as a man of God and a conscientious employer of men, who are happy while working for me ten hours a day. I charge it upon you, and all such as you — it is such sedition that you are creating, that the apostle denounces. Moreover, coming from such novices, leads me to warn you to know more and say less. Your mission, if genuine, is to save souls. Exclusive, sacred, grand work. I say to you, sir, attend to it. Respectfully,

W. T. FAUNCE.

BOSTON, June 30, 1890.

Mr. Banks said he did not read the letter because he was in any way offended at this gentleman for his frank statement of opinion, but because it illustrated a certain erroneous sentiment concerning the proper range of pulpit discussion. The phrase "to save souls," has been made to cover a multitude of selfish sins. "When I was in Seattle in the days of the anti-Chinese riots, and denounced the murders of the Chinamen from my pulpit, I was piously advised to devote myself 'to saving souls.' When in Boise City, Idaho, I denounced the growing disposition to cringe to the Mormon sentiment there, some of the time-serving political newspapers severely reminded me it was my business to 'save souls.' And now in Boston, when I denounce the cruel combinations of capital which defeat honest and free competitions in the labor world, and defend the laborer's right to share in the advantages that have accrued from the inventions of our day, I am not astonished to hear the old tune, 'It is your business to save souls.'

"I want it distinctly understood that this pulpit has no mission to disembodied souls. My mission is to preach the gospel of justice and righteousness to men and women who are still in the flesh. A great many men who are made uncomfortable by the conscience-searching truthfulness of the pulpit, would be very glad to turn the ministry aside to dealing with ghosts. If the gospel of the Carpenter of Nazareth has no mission to the carpenters of Boston in their struggle for a just and equitable adjustment of the conditions of their daily toil, then it has no mission at all."

(The foregoing "Sermon Fragments" are gathered from the Monday morning reports of the Boston daily papers.)

MISCELLANEOUS

I

HINDERANCES TO REVIVALS

I SHALL use the term "revivals" in the popular sense, — a time of special and extraordinary concentration of the minds of the community, both in and out of the church, upon spiritual concerns; a time when the whole, or a larger portion, of the church is aroused to the importance of conscious spiritual life, and becomes especially zealous for the conversion of others.

Revivals are, in my judgment, absolutely necessary to the highest and noblest success of the Christian Church. The late Dr. Holland made a statement in *Scribner's Magazine*, in June, 1877, which has been copied into the Encyclopedic Dictionary as a part of the definition of revivals. He says: "Revivals have become necessary to the advance of Christianity, simply because of the incompetency of the ordinary preaching; and the moment the revivals come, the preaching changes, or it changes before they come." I am perfectly in harmony with the criticism on the "incompetency" of much of our preaching to produce revivals. But I do not agree with the sentiment expressed that revivals are unnecessary in a church which has, in the highest and best sense, "competent" preaching.

I am aware of the popular theory abroad that the ideal church is one that enjoys perpetually the revival spirit; where souls shall frequently be converted at the regular public services. I believe in that as far as it goes, with all my heart. I believe that such a condition of church life, though at present rarely realized, is, nevertheless, possible and practicable. The *New York Herald* said editorially, a few weeks ago, that "where there was a pulpit on fire, there would be a crowd of people to see it burn." And if the pulpit is flaming with holy fire, the church will ignite, and week by week some unlighted spiritual natures will be melted down and reclaimed. But such a condition only makes frequent revivals the more imperative, in accordance with the universal law which enlarges responsibility with every added resource or widened opportunity. About such a burning pulpit and glowing church there will be attracted scores, and many times hundreds, of men and women who are drawn by the Gospel warmth and welcome, but who are so chained by the icy fetters of passion and association that what you melt down in the one or two hours on the Sabbath, is congealed again, with the added ice of worldliness, in the six intervening days of the week. But the revival comes, and the combined heat of the whole church is brought to bear on these cold hearts; the melting process is kept up day after day, until the thawed and penitent soul exclaims, —

> "I yield, I yield;
> I can hold out no more;
> I sink, by dying love compelled,
> And own Thee Conqueror."

Buffon, by collocating several hundred small mirrors, and causing the flame of a galvanic battery to play upon their focal centre, melted in two minutes the hardest metals, and set fire to wood at a distance of two hundred feet. So the wise minister who collocates his several hundred Christian mirrors, and by faith, and prayer, and the preaching of God's Word, brings to bear the battery of heaven on their focal centre, has a heat that melts the moral icebergs of his congregation, that he was otherwise powerless to permanently affect.

Now I desire to speak of two classes of hinderances or preventives. The first is in the ministry. There is a class of ministers who believe in revivals, who wish they could have revivals in their churches, but who lack the faith and courage necessary to make them use the methods marked out in the Bible and in the experience of the church, and dare everything in a bold effort to secure a revival. It is said that Admiral Dupont was once explaining to Admiral Farragut the reasons why he failed to enter Charleston Harbor with his fleet of ironclads. He gave this and that and the other reason. Farragut remained silent till he was through, and then said : " Ah, Dupont, there is one reason more." "What is that?" "You did not believe you could do it." And I am convinced that that is the reason why many admirable ministers, in many regards successful, yet go sadly on their way without revivals. Some ministers do not preach with any set purpose of convicting men of sin, or of drawing them to immediate repentance and acceptance of Jesus as a personal Saviour. Ministers who awaken revivals by their preaching, do so *on purpose*, and they make everything bend to that object. They pour the whole flood of their physical, mental, and spiritual energy down the sluiceway which leads to the one wheel that turns the sinful heart in repentance to the Cross.

A young English clergyman, who had preached a learned and logical, but Christless and therefore powerless, sermon, tried to turn aside the searching criticism of a faithful old minister, by saying, " Christ was not in the text." The old gentleman replied: " Don't you know, young man, that from every town, and every village, and every little hamlet in England, wherever it may be, there is a road to London?" " Yes," said the young man. " Ah," said the old minister, " and from every text in Scripture there is a road to the metropolis of the Scriptures — that is Christ. And," said he, " I have not yet found a text that hasn't a road to Christ in it. If I should, I would make one; I would go over a hedge and a ditch, but I would get at my Master, for the sermon cannot do any good unless there is a savor of Christ in it." A revival of tender, but straightforward, heart-searching presentation of Jesus, as the only salvation of sinful men and women, is one of the imperative demands of the hour.

Last year, after a Lake Michigan steamer went down in a gale, and over forty lives were lost, it came to light that some of the drowned would have been saved if it had not been for the fact that some of the life-preservers were filled with grass instead of cork. That fearful cheat was possible because the grass is cheaper than the cork, and the substitute had secured somebody's approval. The grass "preserver" becomes saturated in about an hour, and is then a burden to the shipwrecked human being who has been deceived into the fearful experiment. Miserable a cheat as that was, it is not more miserable than the Christless gospels by which it is, in some quarters, proposed to float immortal souls amid the gales of care and sorrow, of life and death. Only on the bosom of the crucified Redeemer is there a safe refuge.

Another hinderance, which lies at the foundation of the whole question, is the frequent lack of a democratic spirit in the church. There is, in all our churches, a constant tendency toward an aristocracy of some kind. It may be money, or brains, or social standing, or something else, but that tendency has to be contended against everywhere. Churches under the domination of an aristocratic spirit do not have revivals. The reason is not hard to find. Such church aristocrats get practically to have a creed like this: "Some souls are very valuable; the souls connected with our set most valuable of all. It would be a great calamity if the son of Dr. Longpurse, or the daughter of Banker Bigwallet, or the brother of Professor Goldspectacles, should go to the bad and be lost, but the common crowd are of a different order of being."

Some of these good aristocrats would go a little farther, and open their plethoric pocket-books to help send an evangelist to preach the Gospel to the "common people" in some mission chapel. But the idea of using their aristocratic temple, with all its elegant appointments, as a battle-ground for the souls of the perishing masses, never seriously occurs to them. Now, churches do not have revivals while the members feel that way. The revival spirit is not contagious among that class. No vaccination was ever a more perfect refuge against smallpox; they are not in danger of even the varioloid.

Revivals do not come until a church is imbued with the conviction that an immortal soul is worth more than anything else on earth, and that it is as great a calamity in the sight of God that the hack-driver's son or the washerwoman's daughter should go wrong, as the proudest scion of nobility on the foot-stool. Many city churches are languishing for just that influx of new life that would come with a revival of the democratic spirit, which would give the working people a welcome, with a warm human sympathy that would overcome the wide-spread conviction among them that they are not wanted.

Many churches do not have revivals because they have settled down into a sort of religious club-life, and are congratulating one another that they are having a comfortable, soothing journey from suburban villas to glory. Oh, for some flash of heavenly lightning to awaken such churches to the fact, as Hugh Price Hughes well puts it, that "the mission of the church is not to coddle saints, but to collar sinners!"

The *Methodist Times* of London tells a good story of an aristocratic brother who did not propose to be jostled, either physically or spiritually, by the common people. A few years ago, a most successful Wesleyan missionary was stationed at a stately old chapel in the west of England. On the first Sunday morning he found a poor congregation, and instantly decided to mend it. He proposed an out-door service before the evening service, and, of course, found all the young people ready to follow him. The result was, that in the evening the chapel was full. On the next Sunday night it was crowded. The next day was the quarterly meeting. When the business of this meeting was cleared away, an elderly and very reverend-looking trustee addressed the meeting. He wanted to know whether a new minister had power to do as he liked in holding out-door services. The old man was profoundly moved. He had attended that chapel for forty years; and for the first time in his life, on the last Sunday evening, he had actually been unable to get into his seat.

The chapel was positively full of "common people!"

The new minister, instead of feeling the horror of his position, shouted "Glory!" And he went on to remark that the Conference had sent him there to fill that chapel, and he meant to do it. If the dear and reverend brother who had spoken objected to the common people coming into the sanctuary, he would better go elsewhere where there were no common people, for all the reverend brethren in the world would not deter him from trying to save souls. The dear old man did go elsewhere, and the people were saved. A great revival swept over the community, and the hitherto empty and useless old chapel became the centre of a mighty religious influence. They call that sort of work, across the Atlantic, the "forward movement." May the free winds carry it over all seas, and all our sails fill with the holy energy of the "forward movement"!

II

NOWITKAN, THE HERMIT OF THE SKAGIT

MANY years ago, during the epoch which is characterized by a late writer in the *Overland Monthly* as the "days of barbarism on Puget Sound," there lived in a rich valley on one of the tributaries of the Skagit River a noted and wealthy Indian chieftain named Nowitkan. He was the richest and most influential of his tribe. He was rich in canoes, ponies, and cattle, and carried on a flourishing trade in wolf and mountain-goat skins. He belonged nominally to an Indian reservation, which was controlled then, as now, by the Roman Catholic Church.

The priests of this church had been among these Indians, and had baptized them all into the Roman Catholic communion. They had not, however (and, so far as I have been able to learn, never have, on the Pacific coast), interfered with their polygamous customs, the buying and selling of wives, or, in fact, with any of the heathen and sinful habits prevalent among them.

Nowitkan was a polygamist, having taken wives in proportion as his property had increased. Soon after his baptism into the Roman Catholic Church, he was taken suddenly ill, and to all outward appearances died. The Indians mourned him as dead; but after two or three days of funeral preparations and ceremonies, he, to their great astonishment, came back to life, and told them the following remarkable story: He declared that, as they had supposed, he had really died; that when he went out from the body, he came into the presence of the Great Spirit and held conversation with him. The Great Spirit was angry with him and with his people, and told him he had done very wrong in taking more than one wife. He was also displeased with them for praying to the Virgin Mary, as they had been taught to do by the priests; but told him that they ought to pray to no one except Jesus, who was the Great Spirit's Son, and who would hear them, and forgive their sins. The Great Spirit told Nowitkan that for these and many other bad acts, he could not be permitted to enter into the "Happy Hunting Grounds," but must go away into a strange and unhappy desert. Then Nowitkan pleaded for mercy. He pleaded in his own behalf that he had committed these wrong deeds through ignorance, and promised that if the Great Spirit would permit him to go back to the earth for a time, he would put away all his wives except one, would quit all his wicked ways, and worship only Jesus, God's Son.

When at last this request was granted, he begged that he might be permitted to keep his youngest and prettiest wife; but the Great Spirit had commanded to keep only the eldest, the one he had taken in his youth. To the great astonishment, not only of his own people, but of the early white settlers as well, Nowitkan proceeded at once to put these instructions into practice. He separated from all except his first wife; refused to have anything more to do with the Roman priests or their ceremonies; but lived a very serious and prayerful life. Not only did he change his own habits of life, but began preaching his new faith to the other Indians. He went about gathering them together, telling them his experience, denouncing their sins, and urging them to worship no one but the Lord Jesus Christ.

He attracted great attention among the Indians, and indeed his influence threatened to overthrow the entire spiritual control of the priesthood among the Indians of the Lower Puget Sound. The matter, of course, was speedily brought to the notice of the agent and priest on the adjoining reservation. These emissaries of Rome acted with promptitude, and in perfect harmony with the late defence of the Inquisition made by the wily Monseigneur Capel. They gathered all their assistants, marched on the home of the unsuspecting heretic, burned his canoes, confiscated his ponies, butchered his cattle, and carried him away to the jail on the reservation. For two long years Nowitkan lay in jail. During that time all the arts of persecution and persuasion were in turn used on this self-ordained missionary, to make him recant, but in vain. At last, worn out and ready to die, he promised, if given his liberty, he would leave his tribe and confine his faith to himself; on this promise he was finally released, and, taking his faithful wife, he went into the wilderness up near the foot of Mount Baker, and there lived the life of a recluse. He made his humble livelihood by hunting and fishing; sending his wife into the settlements with his pelts, not daring himself to risk a meeting with the Roman Catholic authorities.

Here, in this lonely hermitage, he was visited, in 1875, by one of our preachers, who is at present a member of the Puget Sound Conference. The minister found him very shy and fearful at first; but when he had succeeded in convincing him that he was not a Catholic, he opened his whole heart to him, and related his history substantially as I have given it here. He reiterated his faith to his Methodist brother, and assured him that during all the years since that wondrous vision, he had not ceased to try to please the Great Spirit, and continued to pray to Jesus, who was, as he termed it, the "Papa's Son."

Whether he still keeps his lonely watch at the foot of gray old Mount Baker, or has gone to his final reward in the "Happy Hunting Grounds," I do not know. I have tried simply to give the record without comment, as related to me, and fully believed by the early settlers, and as consistently maintained through many long years by Nowitkan himself, whom I have thought worthy of a printed remembrance as the Hermit of the Skagit.

[Published in the *Western Christian Advocate*, March 18, 1885.]

III

METHODISM AMONG THE NOOTSACKS

THE Nootsack Indians live on the eastern side of the Lower Puget Sound, far up, close to the British line. There are, all told, about three hundred men, women, and children.

In the days of the Hudson Bay Company's rule, they were visited by some Roman Catholic priests, and taken wholesale — dirt, sins, heathenism, and all — into the Romish Church. No attempt was made to reach their hearts with the spiritual cleansing, and the outward routine of their heathen life went on much as before. So matters stood until a few years ago an intelligent young Nootsack went over on the Frazer River to visit some of his swarthy friends who owed allegiance to Great Britain.

There was among the British Indians a Wesleyan missionary; and the visit of the young Nootsack occurred at the time of their glorious camp-meeting, with the genuine Methodist flavor about it. The power of God fell upon the people. Christian Indians were happy, Indian sinners were under conviction, and repenting Indians were happily converted to God. The young Romanist from the land of the Nootsacks was full of amazement. He had never witnessed anything like this. Soon, however, his amazement changed to terror in his own behalf; and there on the Frazer River campground, the first Nootsack found the pearl of great value. He was now all aflame to carry the "good tidings" to his brethren at home. Charles Wesley's hymn was realized again up in that northern forest, in that Nootsack heart, with all the tenderness ever experienced in city church or by cultured Caucasian.

> " Jesus all the day long
> Was my joy and my song:
> Oh, that all his salvation might see!"

He hurried home, gathered some friends together, and began to tell them his experience and exhort them to repent; but they laughed at him, called him crazy, and left him to preach to an empty wigwam. He followed them about for some time, doing his best to make them hear, but in vain. Finally, he appealed for help to the Wesleyan missionary, who, at his solicitation, visited the Nootsack valley and preached to the people. The novelty of hearing a white man who could speak in their own language was sufficient to attract a fair congregation of curious listeners.

The missionary preached to them "Christ and him crucified." Our young convert was on the alert, watching each dusky face for favorable indications, and praying for God's help. At last he saw the chief man becoming interested, and then a softening in the expression of another old man of considerable influence; then the big tears rolled down their cheeks as they listened to the old yet ever-new story. The young Indian declares that the happiest experience of his life was the sight of those penitential tears. Many of them were converted to God at that time.

One hundred and thirty-five of them are members of the Methodist Episcopal Church, and they have a Sunday-school numbering, on the average, one hundred. They belonged to the Lummi Reservation; but as that is under Roman Catholic control, they have dissolved their tribal relations, have taken land in severalty, and are now receiving United States patents for their homes. They are adopting the habits and customs of Christian civilization. In the summer time, when they go in large numbers up the Sound to work for the farmers during harvest, the most careless employer can easily distinguish the Nootsack Indians from the others. They are noticeable, in the fact that they do not lie or steal, and cannot be persuaded to work on Sunday, no matter how flattering the inducements. They spend the harvest Sabbaths in prayer and class-meetings, and in singing Methodist hymns. There are, among the spiritual descendants of Wesley, many richer in intellect and social culture; but I doubt if any are richer in sincere appreciation of the redeeming love of Jesus, than these sons and daughters of the Nootsack.

[Published in the *Northwestern Christian Advocate*, March 11, 1885.]

IV

PERSONAL EXPERIENCES IN THE ANTI-CHINESE RIOTS

IT was my fortune to be the pastor of Battery Street Methodist Episcopal Church in Seattle, Washington, during the anti-Chinese agitation of 1885 and 1886. As to the causes which led to the cruel and outrageous treatment of the Chinese, I will quote from an article which I furnished *Zion's Herald*, at the request of the late Dr. Bradford K. Peirce, while I was on the ground of the disturbance : —

"A few months since, when the news came of the Wyoming massacre of Chinese miners, there had been as yet scarcely a ruffle on the quiet waters of Puget Sound concerning the now vexed Chinese question. Almost simultaneous with that, perhaps a few days later, there appeared on the scene an Irish agitator from California, who proceeded to harangue the laboring people, and to organize them into secret lodges. It has been the old story over again, of the man who was given a small box in which was confined an evil spirit. In answer to its pleading, he partially opened the box, and out of it sprang a giant which seemed to fill the earth. We had turned loose on us one wild Irishman, and out of his communistic heart has sprung a phantom, whose shadow has darkened the whole northwest coast, and whose tread has made our young city shake with terror.

"Ere thirty days passed, four Chinese laborers had been cowardly murdered in their beds, and a camp outfit worth some thousands of dollars burned at midnight, the inmates being driven half naked into the woods. Within ninety days these so-called *knights* arose *en masse* at Tacoma, and drove two hundred Chinese residents from their homes, through the drenching rain, to a railway station nine miles distant; they herded them on the open prairie, the storm beating all night long on the unprotected crowd, and next morning drove them all into the cars of an outgoing train, except two poor wretches that had to be carried, having died from exposure during that awful night.

"Now, then, let us study a moment the excuses given for this agitation. One favorite rallying cry is that we are being overwhelmed by a great multitude of Chinese laborers, in opposition to, and defiance of, the restriction law. But the census statistics do not bear out this statement. There are only thirty-three more Chinamen to-day, when our population is one hundred and thirty thousand, than there were five years ago when we had only seventy thousand people. If twenty-five white people were able to get along peaceably and prosperously in competition with one Chinaman five years ago, there is no reason to believe forty-five white citizens are in danger of being overwhelmed by the same Celestial at the present time.

"Besides, the cry that the Chinese bring the white laboring classes into a degrading competition with 'cheap labor,' loses its force when we are reminded that there is no place in the civilized world where laborers receive such generous wages, in proportion to the cost of living, as they do here. The one great bar to the general advancement and prosperity of the Pacific Coast section, is that labor is so high that it practically prohibits home manufacture. The butter on our table was made in an Iowa creamery; the lard used to shorten our pie-crust was canned in Chicago; the cheese we eat was pressed in New York; our shoes, made from hides which originally grew on Puget Sound cattle, have twice crossed the continent before they are ready for our wear; the wool sheared from our sheep this season will be shipped back next year in ready-made clothing, with two freight rates added; and other things innumerable might be mentioned. The greatest need we have is the importation of cheap labor, backed by capital, to sustain manufactories.

"Another complaint made against the Chinamen is that they send all their earnings back to the Flowery Kingdom. This is, as a rule, true; after their living expenses are taken out, which, however, are not a small item. Nothing could be farther from the truth than the statement often made that the Chinaman drives out the white laborer by starving himself. The Chinaman has one peculiar characteristic, — he lives according to his income. If he makes only fifty cents a day, he lives on vegetable soup and boiled rice, keeps out of debt, and steers clear of the gout. If he gets a dollar a day, he has beef, pork, potatoes, fish, and wheat bread. And if you raise his wages to a dollar and a half or two dollars, he will eat more chickens, turkeys, geese, and fruits, out of his wages, than any other class of foreigners the writer has yet seen in America. But, suppose the Chinese do send their surplus earnings home, even that is infinitely preferable to the use made of their money by a large class of other foreign immigrants. . . . I am satisfied that if the Chinamen resident in Washington Territory had been as liberal patrons of the liquor traffic as European foreigners, it would have been impossible to have aroused the present agitation."

In the midst of the agitation I preached on the subject from my pulpit. The following quotation from the concluding paragraphs of my discourse, which was stenographically reported for the daily papers, will give the reader some idea of the tension of the public mind: —

"I myself have received repeated warnings that if I did not keep my mouth shut on the Chinese question I should not only receive personal injury, in fact death, but my church should be burned to the ground. Now then, in regard to these warnings I have this to say: I am sent out to preach a gospel that declares that Jesus Christ by the grace of God tasted death for every man. I am sent out to preach by virtue of a commission which says, Go ye into all the world, and preach the Gospel. To whom? To Englishmen, to Americans? To Irishmen, to Germans, to men with white faces and short hair? No. To preach the Gospel to every creature; and may my tongue cleave to the roof of my mouth, and my good right arm fall palsied to my side, before I utter one word or lift one finger to close the door of the church of Jesus Christ upon one single soul for whom my Saviour lived, suffered, and died. It is a little late in the day to undertake to shut the doors of a Methodist Episcopal church because of somebody's race prejudice. Good old John Wesley said, 'The world is my parish.' The Methodist Church was established on that idea. Our missionaries have belted the globe, and preached and suffered and died, that every creature might hear the Gospel. We have buried one of our bishops in Syria, another in China, another beneath the waves of the Indian Ocean; and their brave successors press forward gladly to take their places in sacrifice, in hardship, or in the grave. When race prejudice was bitterest against the black man in the South, the Church never lacked volunteers to follow the lead of heroic Bishop Gilbert Haven, who wrote home in the midst of the struggle: 'The South hate me so terribly that they may take my life. But be it so. The truth will live and win, whether I live or die.' The spirit is not dead. When Bishop Taylor asked for half a hundred men and women to go into the heart of Africa, to go without salary, and to go in the face of certain hardship and probable death, the trouble was not to find those willing to go, but to deny the many who offered. The Church never had a forlorn hope but what there were a score of heroic souls ready to lead it for love of God and love of man. So I say it is hardly worth while to attempt to shut the doors of a church like that, even against the Chinese in the city of Seattle, in the year of our Lord 1885. Church homes are pleasant, and life is sweet; but the Church can afford, yes, a thousand times better afford, to have her temples burned to the earth, and her ministers assassinated in the darkness, than that either the lips of the one or the doors of the other shall be cowardly closed against one single soul, that, abused, oppressed, and defenceless, seeks their sympathy or protection."

At last the storm that had been brewing for months broke upon us. It was a Sunday morning, Feb. 7, 1886. In the early dawn the mob began driving the Chinamen from their stores and dwellings towards the wharf. The governor's message calling upon all good citizens to help put down the riot was brought to me in the midst of a sermon on "Prohibition." I went out of my pulpit about twelve o'clock, and, in company with one of my class-leaders, proceeded to the court-house, enrolled myself as one of the Home Guards, and was given a musket. I did not have the privilege of removing my clothes and lying down quietly to rest, until after the arrival of the United States troops on the following Wednesday night.

On Tuesday evening, when it was rumored I had returned home, my house was surrounded by an armed mob intending to hang me; but I was on guard at the court-house, and my family were at a neighbor's. On the following Sunday a number of men, fearing an attempt to assassinate me at the church (which had been boldly threatened), went early and put their rifles under their pews. Leading church officials patrolled in front of the building, rifle in hand; and I arose that beautiful Sunday morning to deliver my sermon, morally sure that in all that large audience I was the only man unarmed.

V

THE LITTLE YELLOW MAN'S CLAIM ON THE AMERICAN CHRISTIAN

THERE are some phases of the cruel agitation smouldering throughout the Pacific Coast States and Territories, that, however indifferently they may be regarded by the man of the world, cannot but be of intense interest to the sincere Christian. As disciples of Jesus we cannot afford to look at this movement from the standpoint of the ward politician. Any sensible man who has reflected upon the subject, knows very well that if a Chinaman had a vote, these political demagogues who are to-day crying, "Crucify him!" would be crawling on their knees, obsequiously seeking his favor. We should have schemes for controlling the Chinese vote, as we do to-day for carrying the German or Irish vote.

If a jackass could vote, he would be crowned with laurel and fawned upon with blear-eyed affection by these contemptible sycophants. And yet nothing is more astonishing than the extent to which Christian men and women are often influenced by the sophistical appeals of politicians.

For the man whose heart is longing to win redeemed souls from heathen darkness to the Sun of righteousness, there is in these persecutions of the Chinese an all-important question. What influence is our treatment of the two hundred thousand Chinese in America to have upon the efforts being made to Christianize the four hundred millions of Chinamen just across the steam-ferry, in Asia?

This question was specially impressed upon my mind a few weeks ago by reading in a Seattle journal the report of a number of interviews with leading Chinese merchants. It is most pathetic reading. I cannot understand how any true American, whether Christian or infidel, can read it without hanging his head in shame. One of these yellow merchants, Lue King, has lived here thirteen years, has worked hard all his life, saved his money, and invested it all in Seattle, owning real estate and goods worth fifteen thousand dollars. He said to the reporter, "I never saw such a world as this. If the people were going to drive us out, they should have said so before we invested our money here. A great many white men owe us money, and won't pay; what are we to do? I don't think this is right. It looks as if the Chinamen have no protection under the law. While I was in Canton a white man got in trouble with a China steward on board a ship that was in the harbor. The white man kicked the Chinaman to death. Many Chinamen went to the wharf to capture the foreigner, but the captain moved the ship out into the harbor, and they couldn't get at him. The infuriated Chinamen burned the wharf, which belonged to the white man, and burned two houses also belonging to white men. The Chinese government sent troops and captured all the leaders of the mob that burned the buildings, and cut their heads off; and the Chinese government paid the white men for all the property destroyed. But here they burn the Chinamen's property, and then arrest the Chinamen for doing it. They waited till the Chinamen were all killed, and then talked about sending for troops."

What a terrible commentary we are giving this intelligent heathen man upon the comparative worth of our civilization! Gee Hee, of the firm of Wah Chong & Co., who have perhaps one hundred thousand dollars invested in this city, said, "The Americans are not as bad as those from other countries. I think after a while the foreigners will drive all the Americans off the Pacific Coast." There is in this speech of Gee Hee food for a good deal of sober reflection. It is well worth our consideration whether the paupers and criminals of Europe are not a more dangerous class of immigrants than the little yellow men from the Orient. If it be necessary to doubly bolt and bar the western gateway to the sea, is it safe to leave wide open the eastern entrance to the coming of the human sewage of London, Berlin, or Dublin? Shall we violate all the principles of our national history in order to keep the Chinaman out, and carefully hold his place open for the worst of our own race, and welcome them to it with open arms?

The editor of the *Overland Monthly* wisely says that in the cruel persecution of the Chinese we have "simply the savagery of that class of human beings, who, in the midst of every civilized society, especially that of old countries, have managed to remain savages still, possibly more depraved and brutalized by their artificial life in the midst of civilization. Such men come from Europe to our new land abundantly, and become citizens in good and regular standing; they never doubt that, with all their coarse ignorance and brutality, they are by divine right superior to the most learned and virtuous Chinaman or Japanese that ever spent his days and nights in study, or sacrificed his whole fortune to a scruple of honor or an impulse of patriotism."

If you have a heart, read the following, taken from the interviews alluded to above: "In a room adjoining the restaurant was a China boy whose eyes were red and face swollen. The reporter asked him what the trouble was. Foo Kee said, 'Ah Kee has been crying all day. A man told him the Chinamen had been driven out at Tacoma, and some had died. He has some friends there, and he is afraid some of them have been abused and are dead.'" Now remember that these men who are being thus treated came here under protection of the most solemn treaties of the United States Government. They are not criminals, paupers, or vagrants. They are not drunkards, strikers, or rioters. They are quiet, law-abiding, industrious men, whose only crime against mankind is that God gave them an olive-colored skin. Many of them are devoted inquirers after Jesus. At the last session of the Puget Sound Annual Conference, held in Tacoma, there was dedicated a beautiful chapel for our Chinese mission. It was filled with an intelligent and interested Chinese audience. A keen-faced young Chinese gentleman, Mr. Chan Hon Chan, was received into the Conference as an itinerant preacher. This young man was born of a Methodist mother, in China.

and was brought to the baptismal altar of the Church in his infancy. He is a most devoted Christian minister. To-day that Chinese chapel in Tacoma stands desolate. The worshippers are gone. They were driven by an armed mob from their homes. Their dwellings, store-buildings, goods, etc., to the amount of many tens of thousands of dollars, were burned to the ground. And yet this is in Christian America, and under the stars and stripes!

Such deeds are on a par with the expulsion of the Moors from Spain, or the Huguenots from France. Ought Christians to look on in silence?

[Published in the *Western Christian Advocate*, March 24, 1886.]

VI

A SUNDAY WITH THE ANTI-CHINESE MOB IN SEATTLE

SUNDAY, Feb. 7, 1886, will ever be a memorable, if not an honorable day, in the history of the "Queen City of Puget Sound." In the gray dawn, a little band of fifteen men, headed by the chief of police, marched into the Chinese quarter, situated in the heart of the city, and stopped before a Chinese store. The police officer, by virtue of his office, demanded and obtained admission. If you had asked them their business, they would have told you they were a committee, appointed at an anti-Chinese mass-meeting held the evening before under the auspices of the "Knights of Labor," and that their purpose was to see if the "Cubic Air Ordinance" was obeyed. They entered, took measurements, and numbered the inhabitants of the building. Then, coming out, they entered the next building to do likewise. Before the first door could be closed, however, another committee, already numbering a hundred or more, and constantly increasing, pressed in. This second committee was simply a mob. Gathered from the brothels, mines, and logging-camps of the entire Sound, were a great body of men who had been brought together by the secret organization referred to above, for the express purpose of driving out the Chinese. In the early light of this Sabbath morning, while all good citizens were sleeping, the police force delivered the city over into the reckless hands of these vicious men and abandoned women.

Following the first committee, they ordered the startled, half-dressed Chinese to remove immediately to the ocean dock. In order to expedite matters, these self-ordained committeemen began gathering up goods and boxes and placing them upon the sidewalk or street. Soon hacks and drays, previously engaged, began to arrive, and bedding, bundles, and boxes were piled into them and driven to the wharf. Some of the Chinese were awed into quiet submission by the presence of the vast crowd of rough men, and set tremblingly to work to do as they were bidden. These received nothing worse than curses, or at most an occasional kick to increase their speed. But others were not so easily overcome. Some of them were business men, and had accounts all over the city. This was especially true of laundries. Many of the men engaged in the mob were indebted to the Chinamen for washing; some of them from twenty to fifty dollars, and one man seventy dollars. The Chinamen were not allowed to deliver the clothes in the laundries, and by noon on Sunday thousands of dollars worth of clothing had been stolen and carried away by the mob. When these men were brave enough to resist, summary measures were used. Some of them were knocked down with billets of wood, and kicked and cuffed till they were tractable enough to carry their swollen and bloody faces to the wharf after their meeker brethren. Some were dragged from their rooms down a flight of stairs by the hair of the head. One of the noblest ladies of the city tearfully related to me how she saw two men thrown through a window into the mingled mass of mud and stones on the street. One man, a very intelligent, thoroughly educated gentleman, was dragged from a sick-bed, and told to go to the dock. He had been on friendly terms with a local journalist, and he went to him and said, "I am sick. I have been sick for a week, and am not able to go to-day. I am willing to leave. I do not want to live among such people. I will gladly go if I can have a few days to recruit my health and settle my business." His friend endeavored to intercede for him, but in vain.

This man, a cultivated gentleman in every sense of the phrase, in infirm health, was driven to the damp wharf and herded there with the rest, without fire or food for a night and a day.

About the time the congregations in the churches were being dismissed from the morning service, there was driven through the streets of this Christian city, a heathen lady, the wife of a merchant, and richly but modestly attired. Around her was a hooting mob, pelting her with stones, and applying to the shrinking, timorous woman every vile and vulgar epithet that their tongues, long skilled in slimy vocabulary, had learned. She was crying as if her heart would break, and a little rill of crimson blood trickled down from an ugly gash made by a cruel blow on her brow. This scene, remember, was enacted on Sunday, in Christian America, in the year of our Lord 1886!

On sped the hours of that holy day. When the sun went down behind the great white Olympics, there were three hundred and fifty human beings huddled into the damp, wide pen on the ocean dock. Some were stolid with despair, some were sobbing quietly, some moaning in a low monotony of woe; others were quiet from fright, and shrank down beside their little bundle of clothes, all they had been able to save out of years of hard, honest work and self-denying economy.

The darkness of Sabbath night closed down at last with the mob still in possession of the city. This is all I started out to tell you. How the governor's proclamation was read from the pulpits in the midst of the sermon; how preachers and class-leaders, deacons and stewards, answered the call, and marched into line that Sunday afternoon; how at midnight they took possession of the dock, and at midday a little band of less than two hundred stood between their frightened charge and a vicious, yelling, shouting mob of two thousand; how these gallant Home Guards finally rescued the city from the lawless and sustained the law, — all this the quick-speaking telegraph has long since told to all the world. All that and more has passed into history. It was only my purpose to give you a rude outline picture of that awful Sunday, the sights and sounds of which I shall carry with me to my dying hour. No pen can describe, no brush paint in their real colors, the shameful, humiliating deeds of a day which deserves to be remembered among "the days of barbarism on Puget Sound."

[Published in *Central Christian Advocate*, March 3, 1886.]

www.ingramcontent.com/pod-product-compliance
Lightning Source LLC
Chambersburg PA
CBHW031826230426
43669CB00009B/1238